THE REFERENCE SHELF    VOLUME 41 NUMBER 1

# THE
# DEVELOPING NATIONS
## POVERTY AND PROGRESS

### EDITED BY
### IRWIN ISENBERG

*Assistant Resident Representative*
*The United Nations Development Program in India*

THE H. W. WILSON COMPANY
NEW YORK                    1969

# THE REFERENCE SHELF

The books in this series contain reprints of articles, excerpts from books, and addresses on current issues and social trends in the United States and other countries. There are six separately bound numbers in each volume, all of which are generally published in the same calendar year. One number is a collection of recent speeches; each of the others is devoted to a single subject and gives background information and discussion from various points of view, concluding with a comprehensive bibliography.

Subscribers to the current volume receive the books as issued. The subscription rate is $14 in the United States and Canada ($17 foreign) for a volume of six numbers. Single numbers are $3.50 each in the United States and Canada ($4 foreign).

# PREFACE

Before World War II, few people would have cited the economic and social development of the low-income countries and territories in Africa, Asia, Latin America, and the Middle East as one of the world's priority concerns. Today, it would be difficult to omit development problems and prospects from a list of the globe's most critical issues. Indeed, the relative success or failure of development efforts in the low-income countries may well have a greater effect on the remaining decades of this century than any other single issue.

Perhaps the most hopeful factor concerning development prospects is that every low-income country has, at least in principle, made the achievement of substantial economic and social progress one of its major goals. Moreover, the international community has mobilized resources of men and money to assist in this effort. A number of countries—such as Taiwan, Israel, and South Korea—have made remarkable progress in the past decade. Other countries—such as Brazil, Tunisia, and Thailand—have had notable success in developing specific sectors of their economy, though they have yet to solve numerous other problems. Even India, where development problems seem to be overwhelming, has recorded outstanding gains in food yield and industrial production in the last fifteen years. Despite these instances of success, however, the over-all picture for a majority of low-income countries is one of disappointment at the slow pace of progress and concern over the future.

If one truth has emerged from the efforts which have been made in the past two decades, it is that development is a far more difficult process than anyone had imagined. It may, in fact, be the most challenging long-term task man has ever faced. Development issues are not confined to the existence of too many people relative to resources or to food supplies unable to sustain hundreds of millions at an ade-

3

quate nutritional level. In many low-income countries, the very foundations for progress must themselves be built. For instance, it has been necessary to conduct exhaustive soil and water surveys in dozens of nations so that essential information on which to base development plans could be compiled. The most vital services must be expanded and, in a number of countries, created. A cadre of skilled workers in all economic sectors must be built. Power, communications, and transportation facilities must be enlarged to parallel and stimulate growth.

In short, development involves nothing less than the process of nation-building. Considered from this point of view, it is clear that the primary emphasis must be on self-help. If the low-income countries are to achieve a satisfactory rate of progress, they will achieve it mainly through their own will and discipline—though increased amounts of outside help on favorable terms would certainly put them in a better position to realize their goals.

It should also be noted that while it is convenient to speak of the low-income countries as a group, each one of them is unique and has its own set of needs and priorities. In some countries, notably those in Asia, slowing down the rate of population increase is among the most pressing concerns. In other countries, particularly those in Latin America, existing social and cultural institutions may be among the most formidable barriers to progress. And in others, including many in Africa, one of the most immediate needs is for education and training.

It is equally important to remember that there is a vast range of difference in the economic levels of the low-income countries. A few may enter the ranks of the richer nations in the next decade. Some, by contrast, have not moved far beyond a subsistence economy. Some have well-developed industrial sectors and others have no industry at all. Literacy rates are high in some and illiteracy rates above 80 per cent in others

This volume attempts to consider the major issues involved in nation-building and to present a broad view of development prospects. The first section looks at the world as it is today—divided into an affluent minority and a poor majority of nations. The next section focuses on problems in specific low-income areas. The third section offers a selection of articles dealing with the developing world's two most immediate concerns: population and food. The concluding section examines some of the long-term concerns and implications of the development effort.

The editor wishes to thank those who have graciously granted their permission to reprint articles in this volume.

IRWIN ISENBERG

January 1969

# CONTENTS

# I. THE DEVELOPMENT DECADE

## EDITOR'S INTRODUCTION

The United Nations designated the 1960's as the Development Decade, a ten-year period in which the world would marshal its resources and technology for a concerted effort to help the low-income countries help themselves. Although the UN did not present a specific development plan for the decade, it set out target figures in national growth rates and other key areas to be reached by 1970. Though the targets were modest, it is apparent that a majority of low-income countries will not succeed in reaching them. Nor has the UN's hope that the richer countries would contribute 1 per cent of their national income for development purposes been realized. In fact, the developed countries have been channeling a decreasing percentage of their national income into the assistance effort. As a result of these and other factors discussed in this section, the relative degree of optimism regarding development prospects which existed at the start of the 1960's has given way to more gloomy appraisals.

The articles in this section attempt to show what happened—and why. The first selection reviews the history of assistance efforts in the 1960's. The article also surveys the social and political framework in many of the low-income countries and relates it to development issues. The second article, by an international statesman and economist, highlights the disparities between the have and the have-not nations. The following selection focuses on the problems low-income countries face wtih regard to world trade. How can these countries sell more of their products to earn the money with which to purchase goods they do not make at home? The last article is taken from the writings of UN Secretary General U Thant. In this essay he dwells on some of the priority development issues and speaks of the response to low-income-country needs through the creation of new multilateral lending agencies and other organizations.

## AFRICA, ASIA, AND THE DEVELOPMENT DECADE [1]

When the 1960's began, there was great hope that a worldwide campaign to bridge the poverty gap between rich and poor nations could succeed. The poor nations themselves—a number of them in the first blush of independence after years of colonial rule—seemed determined to forge ahead. Many had drawn up ambitious development plans stressing self-help and the need for sweeping social changes.

As for the rich, they seemed ready and willing to help. The United States had paved the way with its mutual security programs of the 1950's, and, spurred by cold war competition, the Soviet Union was following suit. In Western Europe and Japan renewed prosperity had brought an expansion of assistance efforts while multilateral agencies like the World Bank and the UN Development Program were extending the scope of their activities. In short, there was an air of optimism, reinforced by a belief that the rapid advances being made in science and technology would enable developing countries to telescope the modernization process into a relatively short time span.

Against this background, the UN goals set for the Development Decade [the 1960's] seemed modest and entirely within reach. They called for a 5 per cent annual growth rate in national income for the developing countries by 1970 and for a yearly contribution by the rich nations of 1 per cent of their national income to make it possible. "If this can be done," UN Secretary General U Thant said, "and if the population of the developing countries continues to rise at its present rate of 2-2.5 per cent yearly, personal living standards can be doubled within twenty-five to thirty years."

[1] From *Great Decisions 1969*. (Fact Sheet no 3) Foreign Policy Association. 345 E. 46th St. New York 10017. '69. p 25-7. Copyright 1969 by the Foreign Policy Association, Inc. Reprinted by permission.

But it was not done. Today it is clear that many of the poor nations will not reach that 5 per cent growth rate. Some have not even begun to lay the foundation for future development. And, as a percentage of national income, contributions to the development effort by rich nations have actually been declining. Among the developed countries, only France has consistently met the 1-per-cent-of-national-income target. U.S. aid has fallen off to about one half of 1 per cent. Soviet aid is also being reduced. All told, in 1961 the Western countries, Japan, Australia and the Soviet Union were transferring the equivalent of .83 per cent of their combined gross national product (GNP) — total annual output of goods and services—to the developing nations. By 1967, their transfers had fallen off to about .65 or .70 per cent—even though their combined GNP had grown considerably in the interval.

Thus the decade that began on a note of hope is drawing to a close on a note of pessimism. Citing the "climate of fatigue and disenchantment" that has come to envelop the aid effort, U Thant summed the situation up this way . . . : "We are not winning the war on want. The opportunity gap for many, if not most, of the nations and individuals of the world is growing wider, and inequality is increasing." . . .

### Asia and Africa: A Survey

Asia and Africa may be said to represent the heart of the underdeveloped world. Though it lacks a recent history of colonial rule, Latin America, too, is considered underdeveloped. But by Asian and African standards, the 250 million people of Latin America are further along the road to modernization. For example, of the thirty-three poorest countries in the world (i.e., countries with a per capita GNP of less than $100) , only one—Haiti—is in Latin America. Almost all the rest are found in that diverse subtropical region stretching across Black Africa, South and Southeast Asia.

The nations of this area share much in common. Most have gained their independence in the years since World War II and are therefore relatively inexperienced in self-government. Many are so divided along tribal, religious, or linguistic lines that they scarcely qualify as "nations" at all, in the traditional sense of that word. All are severely afflicted by the problems of underdevelopment: illiteracy, disease, poor diets, rapid population growth, primitive methods in agriculture, low levels of industrialization, mounting levels of urban unemployment as the landless flood into the cities and a host of attendant political, social, and economic ills.

India, with a population of more than 500 million squeezed onto territory one third the size of the United States, typifies the general plight of these countries in many ways. India's government has been sorely tested since independence by religious and linguistic rivalries. With a growth rate that would see the country's population double to one billion before the year 2000, India has been in a constant—and sometimes losing—race against hunger. In recent years, substantial headway has been made in raising the nation's food supply. And, thanks in part to more outside economic assistance than any other country, India's per capita national income has almost doubled since independence (from $53 in 1947 to $104 in 1967). Yet, India remains a deeply impoverished nation whose efforts to feed, house, and educate a rapidly growing population are far from assured of success.

Or take, by contrast, the troubles besetting Dahomey, a pencil-thin land of 2.3 million tribally mixed people situated in steaming West Africa. Late in 1967 Dahomey suffered its fourth army-engineered coup d'état in almost as many years, reflecting the political instability that has embroiled much of Black Africa since independence. Tribal rivalries of the sort that led to civil war in Nigeria have also been the key source of Dahomey's political instability. Meanwhile, this Pennsylvania-sized country must rely, mainly on one export—palm oil—for its meager livelihood; and its government must cope with the nation's dire problems on an annual budget of $32 million—about one sixth of what the City of New York spends each year to run its fire department.

## Our Disjointed World

Between Dahomey and India, a multitude of Asian and African nations are struggling to cope with similar problems and crying out for help.

On the face of our planet today [former World Bank President George D. Woods has said] perhaps a billion people live in countries that have modern economies, in countries whose societies are largely agreed on political forms and social objectives, in countries where, broadly speaking, progress toward those objectives is continuous. That leaves more than two billion people living in countries that are still facing the travail of economic and social transformation.

These two billion people, most of them dwelling in Asia and Africa, account for two thirds of the world's population but share only one sixth of its income, one third of its food production and less than one tenth of its industrial output. . . .

However disappointing its results, the Development Decade may nonetheless have served a beneficial purpose. It has shattered many of the myths and illusions in which thinking about development had become tangled. It has given men a more accurate, if less optimistic, understanding of the nature of the development process. In fact, only now in the sober light of experience is mankind beginning to comprehend the difficulties of the task it faces.

The trouble with India and Pakistan, with Brazil and Ecuador, with the Philippines and Ethiopia [economist Robert L. Heilbroner has written] is not merely that economic growth lags, or proceeds at some pitiable pace. This is only a symptom of deeper-lying ills. The trouble is that the social physiology of these nations remains so depressingly unchanged despite the flurry of economic planning on top. The all-encompassing ignorance and poverty of the rural regions, the unbridgeable gulf between the peasant and the urban elites, the resistive conservatism of the village elders, the unyielding traditionalism of family life—all these remain obdurately, maddeningly, disastrously unchanged. [For some of Professor Heilbroner's further thoughts on the meaning of development see "The Revolution of Rising Expectations" in Section IV, below. —Ed.]

And because they remain unchanged or change so slowly, the old concept of development as a simple transfer of capital and technology from rich to poor, until the latter "take off" on their own momentum, must go out the window. Today it is clear that development, if it is to come at all, must come on many levels—political, social, intellectual, and psychological, as well as economic. This is the great lesson that the Development Decade itself has taught. Men have learned that ineffective government, social divisiveness, inflexible rural traditions, or sizable population increases can cripple development plans as surely as any lack of outside aid. As a result, they have focused their attention more sharply on the social and political framework in which economic development must take place.

## *The Social-Political Framework*

What sort of framework have they found? In general, illiteracy, disease, and malnutrition are the lot of men in most underdeveloped countries. Children are often the only form of social security against starvation in old age. Increases in the output of food supplies are often counterbalanced by increases in the number of mouths to feed. Favoritism and bribery are usually rampant in the administration of government. Higher education is too often modeled on the classical curriculum of upper-class Englishmen, while manual labor is often looked upon as socially repugnant. Differences based on language or caste or ethnic origin lead to bloody confrontations in the streets. A steaming, enervating climate drains the last remnant of energy from undernourished bodies. Social discipline, civic-mindedness, and elementary sanitation are lacking.

## *"Soft Nations," Hard Problems*

The Swedish economist Gunnar Myrdal uses the term "soft state" to describe nations afflicted by such conditions. In his pessimistic account of development prospects in South Asia entitled *Asia Drama: An Inquiry into the Poverty of*

*Nations,* Professor Myrdal notes the lip service paid to democracy, equality, and economic progress by governments of the area and the contrasting realities of life.

The dichotomy between ideals and reality [he writes] and even between enacted legislation and implementation, should be seen against the background that India, like the other South Asian countries, is a "soft state." There is an unwillingness among the rulers to impose obligations on the governed and a corresponding unwillingness on their (the people's) part to obey rules laid down by democratic procedures. The tendency is to use the carrot, not the stick. The level of social discipline is low compared with all Western countries—not to mention Communist countries.

Thus, Myrdal notes,

the caste system is probably stronger today than it was at the time when India became independent. And this in turn is largely the result of the operation in a very poor and inegalitarian society of the political processes themselves.

Professor Myrdal belives that irrational attitudes and outmoded institutions are mainly responsible for the abysmally low levels of living in South Asia.

For instance [he writes] there is throughout the region a dislike for manual work, and this affects the way people approach education and the use they make of it. The notion that education is valuable because it affords an avenue of escape from manual work cannot be regarded as legitimate from a development point of view.

The contempt for manual labor has other serious effects. To protect their status and keep their hands clean, landlords and wealthier tenants leave the cultivation of the land to sharecroppers and laborers. The latter, in turn, have little incentive to increase agricultural yields because a large share of any stepped-up output goes back to the landlord. The over-all result is a society top-heavy with economic "drones" who are dependent on undernourished and disease-ridden manual workers at the bottom for their daily bread.

In the face of such internal obstacles, Myrdal discounts the importance of external investments in the development process. As long as the existing social-political framework remains unchanged, economic development will lag and much of the external aid will be wasted. Though Myrdal calls for greater aid efforts on the part of the rich, the most urgent need, in his view, is for internal reform. Yet, he says, internal reform may be long in coming, both because the weak governments of South Asia are a poor match for the development task and because the elites presently holding power find things comfortable the way they are.

### Nigeria's Gloomy Record

In Africa the broad picture is also discouraging. Far from traveling along the road to development, most African states have yet to establish the very underpinnings of nationhood itself. Until they settle their border and tribal disputes and arouse something resembling a national self-consciousness, they will probably remain, in Heilbroner's words, "no more than names insecurely affixed to the map, not social entities capable of undertaking an enormous collective venture in economic change."

The recent history of Nigeria is instructive in this regard. With some sixty million people, Nigeria is Africa's most populous state and territorially one of its largest. When it gained independence in 1960 it ranked among the twenty poorest nations in the world, but thanks to an enlightened British colonial policy it had a nucleus of trained civil servants and politically sophisticated leaders. With substantial outside assistance, these men set out to make Nigeria a showcase for African development and democracy. In 1962 a carefully devised six-year development plan was launched, and Nigeria became one of the major recipients of U.S. aid on the continent. By 1965 the nation was being hailed as Africa's "best hope" for progress under democratic auspices.

Yet from the start Nigeria's leaders confronted an ominous problem: tribalism. For the British, Nigeria had been little more than a convenient administrative unit for colonial rule. For the 250-odd tribes that inhabited the country at independence, Nigeria was to become a fierce battleground of rivalry and dissension. In 1967 Nigeria's dreams of development were shattered by a brutal civil war between tribes owing allegiance to Biafra and those loyal to the central government. Before its results could be tallied, the first six-year plan was wrecked on the shoals of political disunity. Africa's "best hope" had become Africa's worst disaster.

## Mounting a Holy War

The findings of Myrdal and the events in newly independent Africa raise some disturbing questions about prospects for progress in the poorer two thirds of the world. Is development possible in the face of what Heilbroner calls "the indifference or incompetence or corruption of governing elites: the incredible sheiks with their oildoms; the vague, well-meaning leaders of India unable to break the caste system, kill the cows, control the birth rate, reach the villages, house or employ the labor rotting on the streets?" Can the deadweight of superstition, tribalism, and tradition be overcome?

There seems to be a growing body of opinion which holds that only out-and-out revolution—the complete restructuring of society—offers hope for a breakthrough.

Historically [write professors J. P. Nettle and Karl von Vorys of the University of Pennsylvania] it is not difficult to show that successful economic development has almost invariably depended on political stability. But perhaps more significantly, this stability has always been based on a new order, established as a result of large-scale, intense and often lengthy violence.

Heilbroner carries the thesis a step further. Citing communism as the "great modernizer" of this century, he wonders aloud whether Communist revolutions might not, in fact, be what is required.

The conditions of backwardness [he writes] must be attacked with
the passion, the ruthlessness and the messianic fury of a jihad, a
holy war. Only a campaign of an intensity and single-mindedness
that must approach the ludicrous and the unbearable offers the
chance to ride roughshod over the resistance of the rich and the
poor alike and to open the way for the forcible implantation of
those modern attitudes and techniques without which there will
be no escape from the misery of underdevelopment.

Only communism, he suggests has shown itself capable of
mounting the "frenzied assault" that is required.

### Is Violence Necessary?

It is true, of course, that since the Communists seized
power in China twenty years ago, an almost nonstop "frenzied assault" has shaken that impoverished country to its
foundations. Yet has China moved any farther along the
road to development than, say India? Indeed, in the wake of
the current "cultural revolution" there are strong indications that China may be slipping behind.

One can argue that, far from contributing to a development breakthrough, Communist rule might actually impede
the development process by fostering those rigidities and
inefficiencies that characterize totalitarian control of economic activity.

What is required in the underdeveloped countries [Professor Milton
Friedman of the University of Chicago has written] is the release
of the energies of millions of able, active, and vigorous people who
have been chained by ignorance, custom, and tradition. . . . These
people require only a favorable environment to transform the face
of their countries. Instead there is real danger that the inherited
set of cultural and social restraints will simply be replaced by an
equally far-reaching imposed set of political and economic controls,
that one straitjacket will be substituted for another. What is required is rather an atmosphere of freedom, of maximum opportunity for individuals to experiment, and of incentive for them to
do so in an environment in which there are objective tests of success
and failure—in short, a vigorous, free capitalistic market.

## THE HAVES AND THE HAVE-NOTS [2]

There is a marked divergence in economic conditions
and standards of living between the industrialized and the
less developed countries of the world. It is the . . . [most
acute] problem of our time and in its gravity transcends all
other contemporary social and economic issues. The older
. . . conflict between social classes, found within every nation,
is now less sharp. Today, the differentiation and disparity
between rich and poor is geographical. . . . It is the discrep-
ancy between the industrialized and developed countries of
the North and the poor and underdeveloped countries of
the South. . . .

The composition of the underdeveloped two thirds of
humanity reveals itself in the following data:

> There are . . . about 3,300 million people
> in the world. Almost 1,000 million live in very poor
> countries; about 1,100 million in poor countries;
> nearly 400 million in middle-income countries; and
> only 800 million in rich countries.

> The 800 million or so inhabitants of the rich coun-
> tries produce every year about seventeen times as
> much as the 1,000 million or so inhabitants of the
> very poor countries. The United States with less than
> 200 million people produces almost twice as much as
> all the 2,500 million people in the non-rich countries.

> The average person in a very poor country has
> an income of about $85 a year; the average person in
> a rich country, about $1,750 a year; the average per-
> son in the United States[,] about $3,000 a year.

> Every year the population of the very poor and
> the poor countries combined goes up by about 50
> million. This is at the rate of 2.3 per cent a year. The

[2] From *Hemispheres North and South: Economic Disparity Among Nations*,
by David Horowitz, governor of the Bank of Israel. Johns Hopkins Press.
Baltimore. '66. p 3-13. © 1966 The Johns Hopkins Press. Reprinted by permission.

population of the rich countries goes up at about
half that rate—1.2 per cent a year. [Escott Reid. *The
Future of the World Bank.* p 61.]

Moreover, almost half of the world's population is still
hungry, or badly nourished, or both. . . . [A] recent conference of the United Nations Food and Agricultural Organization presented the world with a frightening specter
of famine in many underdeveloped countries within the next
ten years, as the rapidly rising population of the poor nations outstrips the increase in food supply. In some of the
developing countries, production of food in relation to population has actually been declining for the last five years.
The reasons for this disastrous retrogression are evident:

> The food problem itself is not new; it has always
> existed. It is the magnitude of the problem that has
> changed. Two factors are responsible. First, the num-
> ber of people in the world is increasing so rapidly
> that it now seems quite likely that the *increase* in
> world population between now and the end of this
> century, only 36 years hence, will equal or exceed the
> current population. Secondly, this is occurring at a
> time when the amount of new land suitable for culti-
> vation is rapidly diminishing. [Escott Reid. *The Fu-
> ture of the World Bank.* p 63.]

The famine that afflicts large areas of Asia, particularly
India, throws the problem into sharp relief in human terms.
The following words of the President of the United States
[Lyndon B. Johnson] foreshadow the dangers and difficulties
inherent in the situation:

Candor requires that I warn you that the time is not far off when
all the combined production on all the acres of all of the agriculturally productive nations will not meet the food needs of the
developing nations unless present trends are changed.

Destitution, malnutrition, and distressingly low standards of living are aggravated by psychological and socio-

logical conditions. The "demonstration effect" of modern civilization and of standards of living superior to those of the overwhelming majority of the people in underdeveloped countries is conveyed to the latter by the media of mass communication—radio, motion pictures, etc. The sociopolitical repercussions of the gap between the two major areas of the world, that is to say, between the industrialized and the underdeveloped areas, are thus magnified. . . . A new approach to the interrelationship between the developed and the underdeveloped parts of the world has become inevitable. The affluent sector of the world cannot remain a quiet island in the midst of a stormy ocean, an oasis of prosperity in a desert of desperate poverty. . . .

There is a rising demand for a share in the wealth of the world. Even under conditions little short of starvation, the problem is no longer purely physical or biological but has taken on a sociopolitical aspect. The sole radio receiver in the village, the rare visit to a movie, the shining motor car passing through an Asian or African village convey the message of a fuller and easier life, beyond the bare struggle for existence, and under conditions that free for other uses much of the vitality now subordinated to the dreary task of keeping body and soul together. This desire to rise above the vegetative level of life is a powerful element of ferment and expectation. The conflict becomes, therefore, what has been described as a "revolution of rising expectations," and crisis has become well-nigh inevitable.

This "revolution" is, of course, fraught with illusion. The paradise of a Western standard of living seems within easy reach, but the grim realities of the situation soon reveal themselves. Acquiescence in conditions of misery and poverty is gone, and the next move remains a mystery. It is true that, given modern technology and the great accumulation of wealth in the Western industrialized countries, it should be possible by importation of capital to shorten the distance which the underdeveloped countries have to travel to reach the stage of self-perpetuating and self-sustained growth. . . .

Awareness of the possibilities and impatience with the present situation lie at the root of the revolution of rising expectations and are leading to a tragic conflict. The explosiveness of these feelings has been most strikingly reflected in events in the Congo, Laos, Vietnam, and Santo Domingo. There is potential for similar conflicts in many other countries of Asia, Africa, and Latin America. The Western world has reached the point where new instruments must be designed to promote the development of underdeveloped nations, with the clear objective of reducing the most serious and glaring examples of the gap between the industrialized and wealthy North and the underdeveloped South of the globe.

A publication of the World Bank [which offers development loans to low-income countries] defines the situation as follows:

In the last fifteen years the total production of goods and services in the low-income countries has increased at about the same rate as in rich countries, at about 4 per cent a year. This is a great accomplishment. But it does not mean much for the average man, woman, or child in the average low-income country. In the first place, even if production per head were to go up at the same rate in rich countries and in low-income countries, say at 4 per cent a year, this would mean an increase of about $120 per head every year in the United States but only about $3.50 per year in India. Secondly, the same rate of increase in total production in rich countries and low-income countries does not mean the same rate of increase in production per head[,] for the population of low-income countries has been increasing twice as rapidly as the population of rich countries. In the past fifteen years the population of low-income countries has gone up about two fifths; the population of rich countries by about one fifth. . . .

The result is that in the rich countries average income per head is going up by about $50 a year, in the poor countries by about $2.50 a year and in the very poor countries by about $1.50 a year. Moreover, in the past ten years the trend in the rate of growth of population in the low-income countries has been upward and the trend in the rate of growth of production has been downward so that the rate of growth in income per head has been shrinking. ⌡

If aid from rich countries to low-income countries is to be decisive, the rich countries must pour into the low-income countries a much greater flow of men, materials, and skills. They must provide more of their aid on easy terms. They must open their markets much wider to the goods of the low-income countries. They must have patience for a long pull. Patience not for a decade of development but for a generation.

Economic growth, however, is primarily a function of investment. Of course, investment is conceived here in its broadest meaning, that is, the investment of capital and skill, of know-how, of managerial ability, and of initiative. In every field of economic endeavor, investment is the key to progress and expansion. The most impressive example of the truth of the statement is agriculture. To expand agriculture and augment the supply of food is the most urgent concern of the underdeveloped world. Yet with the amount of uncultivated land that can be brought under tillage constantly dwindling, progress in this direction is overwhelmingly dependent on larger yields per unit of land, which can be realized only by irrigation, soil improvement, adequate use of fertilizers, and the like, all of them dependent upon input of capital.

The development of manufactures in countries which as yet have no major industries is certainly the function of import and of formation of capital and of skill, as well as of the availability of technological knowledge. There is, however, a remarkable gap between investment in the rich and in the poorer lands. In the underdeveloped parts of the world (excluding China), inhabited by 1.3 billion people, where the need is most pressing, the gross capital investment aggregated $26.9 billion, and net capital investment, after deduction of depreciation, $10 billion. In the developed part of the world, with a population of 505.8 million, gross investment was $162.4 billion, and net investment was $82.7 billion. . . .

The spectacle of such glaring inequality in investment is more eloquent than any other argument or exposition of the case for encouraging the economic growth of the developing nations by means of large-scale investment and influx of capital. It is surely a paradox that the rate of investment is so high in countries with overheated economies, shortages of workers, bottlenecks in productive capacity, and inflationary trends, and yet so limited in countries with dormant factors of production—in particular, the manpower left idle in the aftermath of rural unemployment or underemployment and unused natural resources. . . .

We are confronted by disparities which determine the shape of the world in which we are living today and the shape of the world of tomorrow. The first disparity, already mentioned, is that between the standard of living of the developed and of the underdeveloped sections of humanity, a disparity which, at the extremes, can be as large as thirty to one in average income. The second disparity is that between the political independence and power of the developing states, which today form the majority of the members of the United Nations and which can in some measure shape the destiny of the world, and the deplorable economic conditions existing in such states. A third disparity is that between the challenge which this problem presents and the response to it, which bears almost no relationship to the great objectives of human progress.

## The Politics of Inequality

As a result of these imbalances, the world is seething with unrest, and Asia, Africa, and Latin America are explosive. In less than twenty-five years India, Indonesia, Indochina, Burma, Ceylon, Israel, Ghana, Nigeria, Tunisia, Morocco, the French colonies, the Congo, Cyprus, and many other countries in East and West Africa and Southeast Asia have won independence, in some cases after violent struggle, in others after the voluntary abdication of their imperial masters. The few exceptions, for the most part, are territories where the problem is complicated by the presence in the country of a large minority of settlers from the country of the ruling power.

Despite the achievements in military technology and the enormous military superiority of Western nations, the use of the military machine to preserve and perpetuate colonial domination has become a rare occurrence, and the voluntary transfer of power to the peoples of colonial territories is today more the rule than the exception. However, the position of the West in these free but underdeveloped countries has been weakened by the attachment of the former colonial powers to the social, political, and economic status quo. In the international arena there are many forces discontented with the status quo and strongly attracted to the dynamic power of the East [i.e., the Soviet Union], with its proclamation of the need for radical change and reform. The newly independent peoples are in no position to determine whether the totalitarian challenge represents real progress or whether there are other and better ways, involving less sacrifice, of reaching the desired goal. The West has insisted, over a long period, on the maintenance of the status quo and has attempted to prove that the expansion of the Eastern bloc and its penetration into new areas in effect represent acts of aggression. This attitude frequently has been linked with active support for established social and economic patterns in the state concerned. . . .

The crucial problem of development in the emerging countries is, in its very essence, political. These nations are deeply indoctrinated with the idea of the struggle against "colonialism." Although colonialism as a system of economic exploitation by means of political domination is today a dead issue, and the industrialized nations, with few exceptions, have found it well worth their while to disengage themselves from colonial liabilities (Britain, the Netherlands, and France are good examples), the emotional idea of anticolonialism is as alive as ever. It represents one of the great myths of our time and is a formidable political and spiritual force.

In this century, economic imperialism has outlived its usefulness. In practice, any advantage the possession of colonies may at one time have had for the metropolitan country involved has as good as disappeared. The loss of Indonesia did not in any way impair the viability of the Netherlands, whose subsequent economic recovery was one of the most spectacular in Europe. West Germany, of course, which has no colonies at all, represents the most striking instance of economic recovery since the end of World War II.

Colonialism, then, is dead as an important factor in the life of European nations. . . . Any resistance to the emancipation of the underdeveloped nations which may still exist in the highly industrialized states which once controlled colonial empires is being undermined, not only by ideological erosion, through the progress of democracy and humanism and the political considerations inherent in the cold war, but also by the economic futility of colonialism.

In short, the political liberation of colonial countries is approaching its conclusive stage. However, the old notions of colonialism and anticolonialism still cast their shadows over the next historical goal. That goal will be one of economic growth and development in cooperation with, and by a flow of capital from, the industrialized nations. Unfortunately, the road to that goal is obstructed by an undergrowth of political ideologies and conceptions produced by quite different economic and social conditions. Inertia is largely responsible for this, and is likely to continue until the new trends behind economic and social change become the subject of realistic and acceptable analysis. . . .

What the former colonial countries want is not only freedom from domination and fear but also freedom from want, hunger, and economic insecurity. In the last decade, demographic expansion in the underdeveloped countries accelerated side by side with a worsening of economic conditions due to the decline in the prices of [exported] primary products. Under these conditions, the nations liberated from colonial regimes developed high expectations, with, of course, political independence at the top of the list. But political independence and sovereignty were not enough to solve fundamental economic and social problems. They could do but little to prevent further stagnation and an increasing decline in the standard of living. Slogans left over from the struggle against imperialism were seized upon as substitutes for practical measures to ease an economic and social distress that was rapidly becoming more and more grave. It is significant, therefore, that at a time when the political liberation of colonial countries was taking place at a faster rate than at any other period in history, the nations thus freed had to fall back on anti-imperialist slogans as a kind of outlet for their deep disappointment with the reality of their sovereignty and dawning national maturity.

The struggle of these nations for economic viability and independence, however, has little, if any, relevance to the old notions of anticolonialism. In such a struggle, not further disengagement but deeper involvement of industrialized states in the development and economic growth of the underdeveloped nations is required. Not only independence but also a much greater degree of interdependence is called for.

## "SCANDAL OF THE CENTURY": RICH AND POOR [3]

The first general confrontation between rich and poor nations over the ever-worsening plight of the have-nots took place in Geneva more than three years ago [in 1964]. After three months of conclave, 122 countries produced a series of ringing manifestos calling for new patterns of production and trade, the stabilization of commodity prices at a higher level, preferences in wealthy markets for the manufactured products of the poor, more aid, a new international division of labor—in short, a global redistribution of wealth.

Known as UNCTAD (United Nations Conference on Trade and Development), the North-South confrontation

[3] From article by Arnaud de Borchgrave, senior editor. *Newsweek.* 70:38-40. O. 30, '67. Copyright Newsweek, Inc. October, 1967. Reprinted by permission.

was turned into a permanent institution, which was head-
quartered in Geneva, and now has a staff of some two hundred experts. It spawned a plethora of committees, sub-
committees, working parties and expert groups that have
been meeting daily ever since, churning out millions of
words on everything from food substitutes to a draft agreement fixing the international price of cocoa. But despite all
this, the developed countries are yet to take a single positive
step in the direction of UNCTAD's recommendations.

At first, the More Developed Countries (MDC's) told the
Less Developed Countries (LDC's) to wait for the results of
the Kennedy round [concerning tariff reductions]; benefits,
they promised, would accrue to all. The Kennedy round
ended successfully this year [1967] but once again the poor
were disappointed. There was nothing in it for them and
it has already been bitterly dismissed as "one more scheme
to make the rich richer."

## Huddle

Earlier this month [October] the Asian have-nots met in
Bangkok, the Latin Americans in Bogotá and the Africans
in Algiers, before all coming together in Algiers last week
to prepare for the second big North-South confrontation in
New Delhi next February [1968]. [This conference, known
as UNCTAD II, was held but produced few gains for the
low-income countries.—Ed.] Next month the Western haves
will huddle in Paris and the Communist haves in Moscow
to do the same thing.

In Algiers, President Boumedienne keynoted the open-
ing session of the "Group of 77" (actually 86) LDC's when
he said that "Europe and the United States have plundered
the natural wealth of the Third World." The advanced
countries, he added, "are veritable octopi whose tentacles
are drawing ever tighter on the developing world . . . and
we should consider whatever contribution the industrialized
countries make as a simple restitution of a tiny part of the
debt the Western countries contracted by their odious ex-

ploitation." And with this, Boumedienne called on the poor to battle the rich in a new class struggle.

Though Boumedienne's revolutionary trumpeting had little appeal to the other nations, minister after minister, speaking in the olive-green upholstered Palais des Nations on the seashore eighteen miles west of Algiers, vented his spleen on the callous rich of the North. Senegal's Habib Thiam said: "Deterioration of our terms of trade is nothing but a plundering of countries that produce primary products by those who sell them manufactured goods." Madagascar's Jacques Rabemananjara said the present world economic order "is a source of perpetual misery. It is the scandal of the century." Peru's José Antonio Encinas del Pando: "We came here because the haves won't let us into the twentieth century." Liberia's Minister of Commerce A. Romeo Horton put it this way: "The removal of inequities between rich and poor is the key question of our time; it will decide the issue of war or peace."

Hyperbole aside, there is no brooking the fact that while LDC needs have been growing, MDC efforts have been faltering. Moreover, what passes for Western aid often has precious litle to do with helping the economic development of the needy nations. Aid, in fact, has become a gigantic shell game, with the haves resorting to the most dubious tactics to prove they are meeting the UN target of 1 per cent of their GNP. "Suppliers' credit" from private Western firms at 10 per cent interest, for example, is categorized as aid. When the United States unloads surplus military equipment on an LDC which, in turn, adds to that country's economic burden, it is also called aid. The same label is pinned to money France gives Algeria to compensate Frenchmen and to Germany's reparations to Israel.

Actually since 1961, government aid has remained more or less constant at $6 billion a year. Yet GNP's are up 30 per cent for the West as a whole. Total net outflows—including much phony aid—have declined dramatically in relation to GNP, from .87 per cent of GNP in 1961 to .72 per cent in

1965 to .62 per cent in 1966 to an estimated .55 per cent in 1967. According to [former] World Bank president George Woods, "the available amount of international development finance is falling further and further behind the economic capacity of high-income nations to provide it, and further and further behind the capacity of developing countries to use it productively."

### Closed Circuit

The UN Decade of Development has been an unmitigated disaster so far. There is growing frustration, growing hunger and growing violence. Everything appears rigged against the have-nots, from the technology of the MDC's (whose increasingly sophisticated synthetics reduce the demand for primary products, and whose new production methods cut down on raw-materials consumption) to patterns of trade and lending habits. More and more, the rich tend to live in a closed-circuit, technological economy in which the revolution of rising expectations plays the role of intruder. Perhaps more disturbing, they have little sense of guilt.

When it comes to arms sales, however, all the major powers are very generous. Interest-free, long-term loans are no problem; the buyer only pays for two thirds of his military purchases, the last third usually being written off as a grant and counted by the benefactor as munificence in the yearly reckoning. Since 1950, the United States has sold $37 billion worth of surplus arms and has $15 billion in outstanding orders. "It's as if the big powers have concluded that war among themselves is no longer possible," wrote Béchir Ben Yahmed, the editor and owner of *Jeune Afrique,* "and that the future belongs to local wars whose theatre of operations can only be the Third World, and have therefore embarked on a race to arm the poor countries."

Forgetting for a moment this vast traffic in arms which is counted as economic aid, here are some alarming and depressing facts and figures:

The public debt of ninety-seven recipient countries has gone from $10 billion to $45 billion in a decade. And if the volume and terms of lending remain unchanged—if anything, the terms are hardening—the net benefit to the poorer countries (incoming minus outgoing payments) will fall to near zero by 1975. In the next twelve years, for example, India, which includes almost one sixth of the world's people as well as over half the people who live in democratic countries, will need $18 billion in assistance—$14 billion just to service debts, $4 billion in genuinely new aid. No less an authority than Woods sees the gathering storm of a global economic crisis.

In West Africa in recent years the price of a ton of merchandise imported from West Europe has gone up 25 per cent while the price of West African exports on European markets has dropped 4 per cent. A machine that could be bought for 10 tons of cocoa now costs Ghana the earnings of 25 tons of cocoa.

The LDC's share of world trade has dropped from one third to one fifth in the past ten years. The earnings of the twelve rubber-producing countries have declined more than $4 billion in six years due in large part to synthetic production in Western nations.

The United States ties most of its aid to Buy America purchases. The average for all donor countries is 60 per cent. This raises the price of goods that could have been obtained cheaper from competitive sources. The British openly admit they get back $1.50 for their own industry on every dollar of aid.

IDA (International Development Association), the World Bank's eighteen-member affiliate that caters to the neediest of the needy, is broke. Eighteen months ago [May 1966], George Woods asked member governments to raise their contributions from $250 million to $1 billion a year (the United States contributes 40 per cent). Washington agreed to reach this target by 1970 but wanted the new loans "donor-tied." Woods argues—as do most experts—that only competitive bidding gives the LDC's fair value for their money, otherwise aid becomes a hypocritical misnomer, a disguised subsidy to domestic manufacturers in the export business. The Europeans also like the idea of "tied" aid but are unwilling to match the U.S. contribution. Woods argues that it should all be untied, multilateral aid—or nothing. The LDC's, once again, are the victims of the rich men's deadlock.

There are now 200,000 new mouths to feed every day—or a gain of nearly 70 million a year, about 200 million more since the first UNCTAD conference in Geneva three years ago [1964]. By the time today's twenty-year-old reaches his thirtieth birthday, there will be 700 million more people in the world; when he is thirty-five, a billion more; and when he is still in his prime at fifty-three, the world population will have more than doubled to almost 7 billion.

If present trends continue, the developing countries' food shortage will grow from 16 million tons this year [1967] to 42 million in 1975 and 88 million tons in 1985. And compounding the tragedy, North America's ability to feed the world can no longer keep pace with the ever-growing needs of the hungry.

LDC growth rate comes down from 4 to 2.5 per cent once population growth is taken into account; if petroleum is removed from the growth charts, LDC's advance at a rate of only 1 per cent a year. Countries with a per capita income of $100 are adding $1 per capita for 365 days of labor.

When America and Russia were waging a struggle for influence in the underdeveloped world, aid to the underdeveloped nations was top priority. In return, the great powers expected support for their foreign-policy objectives, or at least, a certain diplomatic gratitude. Just as both powers became disenchanted with the high cost of insignificant political returns, China hove into sight flying the standard of the downtrodden, nonwhite masses everywhere. Once again Russia and America had to give high priority to foreign aid, not to fight one another, but to check China's growing influence. China dangerously overplayed its hand everywhere, got kicked out of most African countries, lost Indonesia, antagonized most of Asia—and Western aid automatically slid down the ladder of priorities. As Algeria's Boumedienne said in Algiers last week, the LDC's are the victims of peaceful coexistence between the two superpowers.

But even when there was a strong political will to help the have-nots, their behavior was often exasperating to the great powers. India and Pakistan, for example, went to war over Kashmir, an obscure issue whose significance few Americans can grasp—and their development programs were seriously hindered. The stop-go chaos and anarchy of the Congo is not much of an incentive for Belgians to continue pouring $70 million a year (and 2,000 experts) into technical assistance for their former colony. Many of the LDC's are small, inefficient units, all insisting on duplicating the trappings of a modern industrial state, from a steel complex and jet airliners to thirty-odd cabinet ministers and government departments, from an army, navy and air force to a network of costly embassies around the world. And the larger national units—e.g., Nigeria, the Congo, India—tend to fall prey to centrifugal regional or tribal forces.

Criticism is rife in Western countries about the have-nots' obsolete administrative machinery, about their inability to adapt technology to rural development or to prosecute education vigorously at all levels to train manpower for the introduction of technology.

Much of the criticism is valid. But the motivation is highly suspect. For the simple, tragic fact is that the rich need the poor and their commodities and raw materials less and less. There are now synthetics and artificial substitutes for almost everything. Thus like medieval landowners, the MDC's are pulling up the drawbridge, hoping that the moat is sufficiently wide to protect them from the serfs, or LDC's.

Dr. Raúl Prebisch, [formerly] UNCTAD's energetic Argentinean Secretary-General, who circles the globe the way most people commute to work, has labored for years to establish a dialogue between rich and poor, although he is painfully aware of Western disinterest. While recognizing that radical measures are long overdue, he has opted for "the slower but surer pursuit of the negotiable and therefore attainable."

Indeed, Prebisch has maneuvered haves and have-nots into negotiations on issues that now have a sporting chance of adoption. The present priorities:

Temporary universal preferences for the entry into advanced countries of manufactured and semimanufactured goods from the developing nations. At Punta del Este last April [1967], President Johnson said the United States was now willing to explore the possibilities of granting temporary preferential tariff advantages to all LDC's in the markets of all MDC's. . . .

Item-by-item stabilization of commodity prices. Only five commodities afford opportunities for international price-fixing as a means of boosting—or at least guaranteeing—the export earnings of LDC's. Agreements already exist for coffee and tin. That leaves tea, cocoa, and bananas. But they only account for 4 per cent of total LDC exports.

A cocoa agreement is now shaping up and will probably be finalized before the New Delhi conference. In the last six months, the price of cocoa has fluctuated between 32 and 21 cents a pound. Under the proposed price-fixing, it would be allowed to oscillate between 22 and 28 cents.

An international insurance scheme to offset fluctuations in commodity prices by providing supplementary financing, thus making possible long-range economic planning, is also being discussed. It would, however, require $300 million or more a year.

These would not be momentous concessions, but they may be the best the LDC's can get. And in Algiers, there was evidence that a new sense of realism was emerging. As Ghana's F. R. Ayeh put it: "Our requests should not be reasonable but practical." Syria's Zuhayr al Khani said the LDC's should make a concerted effort to step up trade between the poorer countries, thus eliminating the rich intermediary nations.

Moreover, the picture is not all black. There are, mercifully, a few shades of gray, notably in Latin America. Government revenues have increased 22 per cent in the last three years, exports are up and tax reforms have been achieved in six South American countries. U.S. private investments are also up, from $242 million in 1963 to $457 million in 1966.

Most important, the world can count its blessings that the rich countries seem to be fed up wasting money in power and prestige plays that have little bearing on the economic development of the recipient. Both the United States and the U.S.S.R. would rather see rapid economic and technological advancement in the LDC's than chaos and anarchy. And they both show signs of recognizing that no one ideological system is uniquely capable of coping with the kind of problems mankind faces over the next decade or two. It is too late for a Great Society confined to one nation. The world shrank by half in 1959 with the advent of jet travel; it is about to shrink by half again with the introduction of the SST. A Great Society is only conceivable on a global scale. West Germany made a step in the right direction earlier this month when it suggested synchronizing its aid programs with those of Eastern Europe.

### New Guidelines

The underdeveloped world, like space, is a common frontier. Both must become cooperative ventures. Economic development, not the cold war, political friendships, or power politics, should become the criterion. The new guidelines (as suggested by [United States Ambassador to India] Chester

Bowles): Is aid being used efficiently? Is the recipient government making an honest effort to tax people fairly, to bring about land reform, to root out corruption, to expand its exports, to reduce its rate of population increase, to stimulate individual initiative?

## PROSPECTS FOR PROGRESS [4]

In spite of dramatic improvements in the prevention of disease which over the last decade have added ten to twenty years to the expectation of life in the developing countries, their average still falls by as much again behind life expectancy round the North Atlantic. In particular, the tragic death of small children weighs far more heavily upon the developing lands. In the most highly developed countries, the mortality rate of children up to five years of age varies from 4.5 to 6.3 per 1,000. Yet in Latin America, the rates are five to ten times higher and in Africa, higher still.

One reason for the contrast in mortality rates lies in the disparities in medical services—in medical personnel, hospital beds, drugs and preventive medicine, for instance, in North America, Western Europe and the U.S.S.R. there is generally one doctor for fewer than 1,000 inhabitants compared with one for 6,000 in India, 32,000 in Afghanistan, 39,000 in Mali and approximately 96,000 in Ethiopia. Failure to invest adequately in the control of disease and the promotion of health, together with a lack of coverage by health services of large segments of the population where disease is endemic, has led in many parts of the world to a deterioration of standards of health and sanitation.

Another reason for the difference in mortality rates certainly lies in disparities in diet. Men and women in North America and Western Europe eat on the average about 3,000 calories and 80 to 90 grams of protein a day. In Latin America, outside Argentina, the average falls to 2,400 calories and some 70 grams of protein; in Asia to 2,100 calories and 50

[4] From *The United Nations Development Decade at Mid-Point*, by United Nations Secretary-General U Thant. United Nations. New York. '65. p 7-32. Reprinted by permission.

grams—a level still below prewar standards; in Africa the protein consumption is lower still. But these abstractions give no true sense of the gap—between the steaks and chocolate, the salads and fruit of diets in the developed countries and the bowl of rice, with little variety beyond a change of sauce, which makes up, day in, day out, the food of most Asians.

These inadequacies in diet and medical care are made more intolerable for about 1,000 million people by the desperate standards of housing which they are forced to endure. The major cities of the developing continents all have their densely crowded shanty towns in which 20 to 30 per cent of the city's inhabitants may be living—without water, without sewers, without roads. And out in the countryside the shacks of day laborers, landless men, untouchables and rural unemployed only seem a little less miserable because of their larger ratios of light and air.

The misery of much of the developing world is a progressive misery. . . . On present showing the numbers of unemployed and men and women suffering from hunger and malnutrition will be markedly greater in 1970 than today. It is in the poorer countries that the highest growth rate of population is found. In most of Asia and Africa it is over 2 per cent and rapidly approaching the 3 per cent level. In some of the Latin American countries it has surpassed that level. On present showing there simply is not in prospect a growth in agricultural production sufficient to accommodate this rising flood of people. The world's agricultural production is growing by under 3 per cent per year, and the growth rate is much lower in some critical areas. The continuance of traditional methods in farming has often been the main obstacle to any significant increase in food production. Rapid migration to the cities has further complicated the problem. The rate at which this migration has taken place has often far exceeded the rate at which urban employment opportunities have been increasing, with the result that unemployment has been rising in many of the developing countries. To give one striking example: in 1955 the Indian estimate of unemployment was some 5 million. By 1961 it had grown to 8 million. Even if the planned production targets for 1966 and 1971 are fulfilled, the Indian authorities estimate that unemployment will still rise to 12 million and 14 million in these two years respectively. A particularly disturbing feature in these situations is the degree to which unemployment will fall most heavily on young people. In Indonesia, 50 per cent of the urban unemployed and in Ceylon 80 per cent are under twenty-five years of age.

This phenomenon of urban unemployment may not, in theory, be worse than the semiemployment and undernourishment of the villagers. But in the countryside family and clan give some support. There is a little more spare food; in some regions, there may be hunting and fishing on the side. The city reduces the new migrants to the rawest struggle for survival. Yet it is to the cities they come in a flood which far surpasses in speed the general growth of population. Cities grow, the world over, by about 4 per cent a year. Some of the greatest cities grow at twice that rate. About five thousand newcomers a week move into Rio de Janeiro. The capital cities of tropical Africa have doubled in little more than a decade.

The problems that spring from the dynamism of growth in population, coupled with the added dynamism of urban expansion, are propelled forward by yet another dimension of dynamic change—the change in people's expectations. This factor is no doubt inescapable in an open world of total communication where the richer nations give a daily demonstration of what can be achieved in terrestrial prosperity. But it compels the governments of the developing lands to undertake policies and projects which, in the short run, tend to complicate their already formidable difficulties. In a world where new drugs dramatically reduce mortality from such old enemies as yaws or leprosy or tuberculosis, people clamor for the medical help that sends the population leaping still further ahead of food supplies. In a world

of hope and upheaval, the young men seize the new means
of transport designed to open up the countryside to stream
away from the farms before there is room for them in the
cities and before the farms are producing a surplus of food.
In a world aware of education as the gateway to advance,
parents demand village schools which the youths often leave
with barely a primary education to seek unskilled jobs in urban centers—just the jobs which a more sophisticated industrialization is beginning to abolish. No government of a developing country can escape these dilemmas. But . . . the
impact of all these dynamic forces of explosive change is,
on balance, to make their difficulties more complex and their
prospects more daunting still.

In the relations between rich nations and poor nations,
the market they share is the worldwide market of international trade, and the higher earnings the poor nations must
seek is a higher proportion of the gains made in international commerce. The share of developing countries in world
exports declined steadily from nearly one third in 1950 to
only slightly more than one fifth in 1962. One of the major
targets of international action must be at least to restore the
proportion they previously enjoyed.

The underlying pattern of the world market has not
changed very much over the last century. It was brought into being by the developed nations' need to look overseas for
food, minerals and tropical materials, to invest the necessary
capital to produce them in mines and plantations, in transport and harbors, to recoup the investment out of the sale
of the exported materials and pay for whatever local balance
remained with their own export of manufactures. This pattern of trade left little capital in the local economy, led to
virtually no modernization outside the sector concerned with
foreign trade and therefore did not set in motion local forces
of diversification and growth. International trade, outside
the developed core made up largely of North Atlantic states,
continued to rest on the exchanges between strong, modernized and developed communities on the one hand and, on

the other, weak economies dependent, very often, on a single product. Intensification of trade could only occur between *developed* economies and virtually the whole organization of the trade remained in Western hands. To this day, about 66 per cent of world trade . . . [is carried on by] the developed market economies. They control 94 per cent of the world's shipping and virtually all its insurance. To a very considerable degree, they still control the processing of the materials —underdeveloped nations account for only 4 per cent of the world's exports of manufactures and even this percentage is very misleading. Nearly a quarter of these exports are provided by the one fabulous source of Hong Kong. . . .

The developing nations' three main headings of dissatisfaction are the uncertainty and instability of export incomes; the difficulty of access to developed markets for some raw materials and for any more diversified and processed exports; and the structural bias of the whole market towards the interests of the rich. Between 1950 and 1962, the unit value of exports from developing countries to developed countries fell by 5 per cent—in comparison with 1955 the figure was 12 per cent. . . . This decline was enough, in the case of Latin America, to wipe out the effect of all the imports of public and private capital during the 1950's. At the same time, the unit value of exports from the developed to the developing countries rose by 16 per cent. The terms of trade between the two groups deteriorated by about 18 per cent over the period. The trade surplus of nearly $2 billion that the developing countries enjoyed in 1950 had turned into a deficit of $2.3 billion in 1962. And to this general decline one must add the annual oscillation in prices, which moved, on the average, by 12 per cent a year.

On the issue of access to markets, the principal difficulty confronting the developing countries is that the whole bias of tariffs in the developed market economies (which absorb over 70 per cent of the developing countries' exports) is designed to discourage local processing or growth of industrial exports from the developing world. On raw materials, Western tariffs are low or nil. On semi-processed goods and on manufactures they are much higher. When, even over these high tariffs, goods still force their way in—this is especially the case in textiles—quotas are often imposed to seal off the flow.

Moreover, as developed technology continues to increase in sophistication, yet more substitutes may be invented to depress primary commodity markets further. Some European countries impose internal excise taxes which increase the price of tropical products such as tea and coffee. Existing preference systems exert some distorting effects. Nor should one forget the monopoly of the developed countries of middleman services. Such factors and many others belie any very great hope of securing, without profound changes in approach, the small extra margin of trade the developing nations must command if they are to acquire the foreign exchange required for a 5 per cent rate of growth. . . .

What are the prospects? Some seem good—for some form of supplementary financing [to compensate low-income countries for unexpected drops in export earnings.—Ed.], for the duty-free entry of tropical products and of an expanded list of other primary materials; some are inherently difficult. To reduce quotas and tariffs on cheap manufactured imports invariably exposes domestic industries to new pressure. Often they are old and entrenched, and while there may be clear advantages to the economy as a whole of moving men and capital out of them, the local interests are often formidably difficult to overcome. Again, the export of some primary products is inhibited by the determination of developed countries to protect their own domestic producers. This not only bears specially hard on those developing countries which export "temperate" foodstuffs; certain "tropical" substitutes for temperate products are also bound to suffer. There is, for instance, some overlap between beet sugar and cane sugar, between soya beans and groundnuts and the developed domestic producer is likely to keep the advantage.

Securing remunerative, equitable and stable prices for primary products offers comparable difficulties. In fact, such prices exist only in high abstraction. In practice, their levels, the stocks, the export quotas, the market machinery needed to sustain them, the disciplines they entail on all participants make them formidably difficult to administer. Fixed too low, they do nothing for the producers. Fixed too high, they encourage substitutes and draw new entrants into production. . . . Most of the existing schemes have been fixed in commodities of interest to consumers, and two of them—wheat and tin—depend not so much upon the scheme itself as upon disposals from the United States stockpile. As regards the first scheme of complete interest to the developing countries —the Coffee Agreement—it is too early to say whether the producer countries will succeed in conforming to the fairly onerous and complicated arrangements covering prices, quotas and access on different terms to markets both inside and outside the scheme.

Yet the complexities are probably less important than the larger issues of governmental attitudes. In this respect, . . . [UNCTAD] had a twofold significance. In the first place, it saw an attempt to coordinate the views of different groups of countries. . . .

In the second place, and as a logical complement to this first development, new institutional procedures were evolved to facilitate such negotiations. These were embodied in a form of conciliation machinery designed to secure agreement between parties before a vote was taken in the case of recommendations "of a specific nature for action substantially affecting the economic or financial interest of particular countries." Recommendations on this conciliation machinery have now been ratified by the General Assembly. The conciliation process thus formally adopted represented an innovation of great constitutional significance at the international level, and a further source of hope for the success of the United Nations' efforts towards reaching the goals of the Development Decade. . . .

To meet the needs of developing countries several new multilateral lending agencies have been established, both within and outside the United Nations framework, in the late 1950's and early 1960's. These include the IFC [International Finance Corporation] and IDA [International Development Association], the African Development Bank, the Inter-American Development Bank and the Central American Bank of Economic Integration, and the Development Fund of the European Economic Community. Preparations are also under way for the setting up of an Asian Development Bank [which is now in operation.—Ed.]. With the increase in multilateral lending facilities, the establishment of the United Nations Special Fund and the expansion of activities under United Nations technical assistance [which were merged in 1966 to form the United Nations Development Programme.—Ed.], the proportion of resources which are being provided to developing countries through multilateral channels has increased from around 6 per cent of the total in the late 1950's to over 10 per cent in 1963.

The need for external assistance is not confined to long-term development capital. Developing as well as developed countries need "working capital" to underpin international trade. Between 1960 and early 1965 the IMF [International Monetary Fund] made available $5.6 billion to forty-three members, thirty-two of them developing states. It has also started to operate a modest scheme to compensate primary producing countries for fluctuations in export receipts. However, much of the finance made available by the IMF has gone to developed countries and the general growth in world trade is outstripping its resources. . . .

The total flow of long-term capital must continue to expand if the growth targets for the Development Decade are to be attained. Projections of past trends in export earnings and import requirements clearly indicate an increase in the gap that needs to be financed by external capital.

. . . One cannot say that the future of this essential financing is secure. In spite of the increase in the flow of long-term capital since the mid-1950's, the target set by the General Assembly according to which resource transfers to developing countries are to rise to 1 per cent of the national incomes of developed countries has not yet been attained. In fact, the leveling off in the flow of funds to developing countries since 1961 has set back progress towards the target. . . .

Let us consider the nature of some of these obstacles to development and the efforts to aid in their solution.

The United Nations has already produced a very large volume of information on the explosive nature of the world's expansion in population. The censuses it inspired have shown, throughout the developing world, even a higher growth rate than had been expected. . . .

So far, the United Nations has chiefly concentrated on drawing attention to population factors in the context of economic and social development by means of scientific evaluation and analysis of data. In collaboration with the interested governments it has created three regional demographic training and research centers for Africa, Asia and the Far East, and Latin America for training technical officers, promoting research work in demography and extending demographic advisory services. It has also organized interregional, regional and subregional conferences. It is now going to expand the scope of its work so that it includes questions connected with policies which are designed to influence the size, structure and change of the population. In Asia and the Far East . . . United Nations activities have been extended to include family planning, and . . . [in 1965] a United Nations team was sent to India to review the family planning program and to make recommendations for accelerating it within the context of the five-year economic plan.

The population problem of the developing countries, however, is not merely one of too rapid increase in the total numbers—it is vastly accentuated by massive and overabrupt shifts of population from the countryside to the burgeoning cities.

The great cities of the affluent world themselves suffer from overcrowding, social disorder, pollution and traffic congestion. But in the developing world, the worst aspect of the urban dilemma is again one that the developed world to some extent escaped—the massive movement of rural migrants into the cities ahead of any real chance of their earning a living. The most conspicuous problem is the acute shortage of housing resulting in overcrowding, the growth of "shanty towns" and a chronic shortage of community services and facilities.

The United Nations has set targets for housing in the developing countries based on a standard of ten new dwellings for every 1,000 inhabitants. So far only two new dwellings for every 1,000 inhabitants have been built in many developing countries even though these countries have allocated 15 to 25 per cent of their total investment in capital formation to residential construction. In the building sector alone systematic and intensive research and action are needed in order to reduce costs, redistribute investment, rationalize technology, expand and improve the building materials industry and devise new financial arrangements to meet the needs of low-income groups.

The United Nations has made studies of urbanization in various regions—Africa, the Middle East. It has called conferences on such issues as new towns and on urban development, planning and policy. It has assisted in the preparation of national physical plans, including master plans for cities. It has helped in resettling shanty town dwellers. The needed statistical information is being assembled. Now the [UN] Social Commission has adopted a proposal suggesting that a full-scale intergovernmental program for joint investigation of the problem should be launched, and areas set aside for studies and experiments in *regional* solutions which seem essential if unwieldy movements of internal migration are not to throw intolerable strains on young and still unstable economies. There is the germ here of the kind of world process of confrontation and education that has occurred in the field of trade; but what is also needed is action and investment on a scale hitherto quite unknown.

Recognition of these deeper difficulties should help to educate and reassure those in the developed world who despair too soon, who fear that because the developing nations have not made a decisive breakthrough to growth and economic independence in ten years, they never will.

But it is also vital to point out that some of the discouragement has arisen from the fact that the slow but real progress of development has attracted less public attention than its occasional spectacular mishaps. Indeed, the public has been largely ignorant of what has been learned in the last fifteen years in the field of development and of how much, in region after region, is beginning to go modestly well. . . .

Much of the progress that has been made . . . and which the Decade of Development seeks to dramatize—is concerned with producing a better soil in which the assistance can germinate. A few examples of this better developmental husbandry will illustrate the point. There can hardly be a realistic plan for expanding a country's infrastructure—transport, power, and so forth—unless an inventory of its resources and their whereabouts has been established. In this field of preinvestment surveys, the [UN] Special Fund has taken the lead. But the greatest potential resource of any country are its human resources. Trained men for administration, for education, for public health and medicine—these, too, belong to the stage of preinvestment since no investment can succeed without them. Here, aided by increasing resources from the Special Fund and the Expanded Programme, the United Nations family is setting up institutions for administration, managerial and industrial training and is supporting universities and technical colleges.

However, far more is needed than the higher cadres. Underdeveloped countries are by definition short of all the intermediate skills as well. A welcome decision has . . . been taken by the ILO [International Labour Organisation] Governing Body as a contribution to the Development Decade, to open this year the Turin [Italy] International Centre for Advanced Technical and Vocational Training. To relate intermediate skills to the probable needs of each particular economy, new techniques have been evolved, particularly the techniques of manpower surveys and educational planning to which the ILO and UNESCO [United Nations Educational, Scientific and Cultural Organization] respectively have made a signal contribution.

And clearly within the context of any educational plan, no single item is more urgent than teaching the teachers. In this field UNESCO with the help of the Special Fund has taken the initiative in planning and establishing teacher-training colleges, and the IBRD [International Bank for Reconstruction and Development, the formal name of the World Bank], recognizing the productivity of education, has begun to provide credits for educational projects which involve the direct development of education itself, both in terms of the number of students in schools and the content of the educational program. Again, UNESCO's recently started pilot program for universal literacy represents an imaginative new approach both to increasing productivity and to the wider enjoyment of elementary human rights and dignity.

No less significant an insight in postwar developmental strategy is the new priority accorded to agriculture. Unless production on the farms—on which the great bulk of the people still live—begins to go up, there is no surplus for saving, no surplus to feed the towns, no surplus to keep pace with rising population and keep down costly imports of food, no agricultural raw materials to feed into industry, above all, no rise in farm income to provide an expanding market for the nascent industrial system. There is no conflict between the priorities of farming and industry, and the need to re-emphasize farming springs not from any desire to "keep developing economies dependent" but simply to counteract the glamor of factory chimneys which may all too often be smoking above products which no one in the community can afford to buy.

Wherever the agricultural sector has been jolted into movement—in Taiwan, for instance, or increasingly in Pakistan—the reasons tend to be the same. Access to water, access to the new technologies of fertilizing and improved seed, ample credit for the farmers, inducements to work and produce more in the shape of land ownership or secure tenancy, cooperatives to give advantages of scale and some control over marketing, quick access to the urban market, reclamation of land through malaria eradication—these are the recipes and it is in these fields that the relevant international agencies, with FAO [Food and Agriculture Organization] at the center of the picture, are at work.

Moreover, each element is seen more and more as a part in a fully concerted policy.

In order to set in motion the forces that lead to an increase in agricultural production and the most effective use of the savings thereby generated, new budget and tax policies and new institutions ranging from those normally referred to as "public administration" to financial institutions such as banks, savings societies, life insurance, and housing associations are needed. These institutions must be rationally organized and staffed and the intermeshing of their work and that of the machinery of government at national and local levels must be ensured. In many of these fields also the United Nations and related agencies are trying to make a contribution, especially through training and advisory functions.

The developing countries themselves have tended to give special attention to the industrial sectors in their development programs. In this field the question of priorities is of particular importance and difficulty. Each country has its own particular endowment of resources and its own local needs and skills. Up to a point, the first efforts in industry usually substitute local products for imports. This is the "beer, boots and bricks" phase through which most economies pass. But whatever the background of the economy, one need is clear—expert advice in selecting the types of industry that are likely to prosper. In view of mounting foreign exchange difficulties in developing countries, projects need to be selected not only on the basis of their potential profitability but also on the basis of their probable contribution to the earning or saving of foreign exchange.

Private foreign investment has an important role to play in industrial development, particularly if, in return for tax and tariff concessions most developing governments offer, the firms are ready to train local people at all levels of skill and look for local participation in the enterprise. While skill bottlenecks in developing countries do impose some limitations on their capacity to make effective use of additional foreign investment, new projects in which foreign capital can be fruitfully absorbed are constantly being revealed and created with the expansion of education and training. The United Nations family is doing its best to help developing countries to identify these projects.

Foundations for what must be done to further industrial development in the second part of the Decade have been gradually laid in the last few years. Within the United Nations Centre for Industrial Development—itself only created in 1961 [and now known as the United Nations Industrial Development Organization.—Ed.]—much progress has been made in different ways towards accelerating industrial development. Of particular significance perhaps have been the studies of program preparation and project formulation, the development of small-scale industries often linked with industrial estates, the broad regional cooperation of neighboring countries in the industrial field, the establishment of a number of industrial technological institutes with the help of the United Nations Special Fund. . . .

In addition to these problems, a new and formidable one —the full dimensions of which are only gradually becoming apparent—looms ahead: this is the problem of the growing indebtedness of the developing countries, and the limits that this imposes on their ability to utilize the credits which may be available to them.

According to IBRD estimates, the public and government-guaranteed debts of thirty-seven developing countries rose from $7 billion in 1955 to $18 billion in 1962, interest payments increased nearly fourfold, and amortization payments were more than tripled. By 1963 the servicing of the external debt absorbed over 13 per cent of the export receipts of these developing countries.

In response to the increasing debt servicing difficulties of the developing countries, the United States took the initiative of providing development loans at low interest rates and on easy repayment terms, and other countries gradually eased their own lending terms. The developed countries also cooperated in setting up the IDA as a "soft-loan" subsidiary of the IBRD.

While more favorable terms on current development lending will tend to slow down the growth of debt servicing obligations during the rest of the Development Decade, it must be remembered that the need for external capital is expected to rise year by year up to 1970 if the growth target for the Development Decade is to be attained. The problem of debt servicing, and the terms of international assistance, are therefore among the major issues to be tackled by the international community in the years ahead.

Not all the effects of the policies and activities which have been discussed in this sector will be apparent at once. There have been some clumsy beginnings and uncertain efforts. But the activity, the effort, the learning, the striving, the aspiration are fully as important as the inevitable delays and mistakes. After such energetic beginnings, it would be tragic and foolish indeed if the effort of assistance were now permitted to falter.

## II. WHAT UNDERDEVELOPMENT MEANS

### EDITOR'S INTRODUCTION

This section examines various regions of the globe with a view toward illustrating some of their specific problems and priority concerns. While these articles discuss the more obvious manifestations of poverty and lack of opportunity, they also tend to emphasize the less apparent institutional and cultural barriers to social and economic progress.

The first selection deals with Latin America. The author analyzes some of the major issues facing the countries of this region. He speaks of the importance of trade, the role of private capital, the attempts at regional integration, and the achievements—as well as the disappointments—of the Alliance for Progress. The next article, written by a noted authority on Africa, focuses on the sub-Saharan nations. The author notes that many of these countries have not yet managed to stabilize their borders and that various tribal groups living within existing boundaries often have no unifying sense of nationhood. At the same time, some of these countries lack the most essential preconditions on which to base development progress. The next article adopts a statistical, but nonetheless illuminating, approach to African realities.

The following piece highlights conditions in Indonesia. It illustrates graphically the multiplicity and interrelationship of the economic and social questions which plague low-income countries. The final article in this section presents a view of what has been called the world's worst urban disaster, the Indian city of Calcutta. Here urban problems have reached nightmarish proportions. To some extent, however, Calcutta reflects the crises which have ensnared urban centers in other low-income countries.

## LATIN AMERICAN PANORAMA [1]

The desire for economic development appears to be the most universal aspiration in Latin America today. Traditionally, the area provided raw materials and foodstuffs for the more advanced countries of the Western world and served as a market for their exports. Escape from this semi-colonial position in the international economy has been a slow and frustrating process. . . . Vital foreign exchange earnings have fallen off, in part as a result of increasing African competition in the few key commodity exports upon which most of the Latin American countries depend. The area's share of world trade dropped from 10.6 per cent in 1950 to 6.3 per cent in 1965. Capital shortages and chronic inflation have hindered efforts to industrialize. Latin American governments have encountered great difficulty in meeting massive needs for investment in basic industrial infrastructure. They have also been hard pressed to provide for the social needs of a rapidly urbanizing population. Food production has lagged behind population increase, and the area presents the paradox of countries with largely agrarian populations expending scarce funds on imports of basic foodstuffs.

While further aggravation of these economic problems has largely been stemmed by measures taken in the five years since the inception of the Alliance for Progress [a U.S. supported program for a decade of self-help and assistance to combat economic and social problems in Latin America—Ed.], comparatively little headway has been made in the creation of viable national economies growing at a rate sufficient to satisfy substantial demands for social justice. . . .

### Economic Trends

The annual average Latin American per capita gross national product (GNP) of approximately $330 is little more

[1] From pamphlet by Ronald M. Schneider, associate professor of government at Columbia University. (Headline Series no 178) Foreign Policy Association. 345 E. 46th St. New York 10017. Ag. '66. p 21-31. Copyright 1966 by Foreign Policy Association, Inc. Reprinted by permission.

than one tenth of that enjoyed by the United States and only one third of the Western European average. On the other hand, it compares quite favorably with that obtaining in the Middle East and is several times higher than the figures attained by African and Asian countries. Among the countries of the region, the degree of underdevelopment and the average per capita income vary greatly. The gross product of the area grew at a rate of 4.7 per cent during the 1950's, but progress from one country to another was very uneven. The GNP's of Brazil, Venezuela and Mexico all grew at well over 6 per cent annually, while in Chile, Peru and Argentina they were expanding very slowly. Moreover, with annual rates of population increase ranging from about 1.5 to 4.0 per cent, some national economies must develop more than twice as rapidly as others in order to achieve any net economic growth at all.

Neither per capita incomes nor annual growth rates are more than crude indicators of levels of living within the various Latin American countries. Distribution of wealth varies greatly. In one country a small elite receives an exceedingly high proportion of the national income, while in another a relatively balanced occupational structure, progressive taxation and social welfare programs lead to greater equality. Almost without exception, however, rural levels of living are far below those of the urban areas, including slums. And above all, nearly half the total population of Latin America still exists at the subsistence level.

In general the larger and more populous countries of Latin America are beginning to pull away from the lesser states in terms of economic development. This is particularly evident in the industrial realm. Brazil, despite a very large rural population and a relatively late start in industrializing, has become the leading manufacturing country of Latin America. Mexico, which has paid greater attention to its rural areas and to social justice, has shown perhaps the most sustained and balanced economic development of any Latin American country. Argentina, which was first to establish the basis for an economic "take-off" but has stagnated since the early 1950's, still has one of the region's highest living standards. Venezuela has made very substantial strides during the past eight years in spreading the fruits of its high oil revenues more widely. Chile and, to a lesser extent, Colombia are also above the region's average in terms of per capita GNP. So is Cuba, despite an absolute as well as relative decline since the Castro regime took over. Peru is the only major Latin American country which has lagged behind in economic development; it is also the only one of these eight nations with a large Indian population. Among the less populous nations, Uruguay, Costa Rica, Panama and the British Commonwealth countries have reached relatively high income levels. The other small countries are truly underdeveloped, with Bolivia, Paraguay and Haiti lagging well behind the Central American countries, Ecuador and the Dominican Republic.

## Foreign Trade and Regional Integration

The United States is by far Latin America's chief trading partner, purchasing over 40 per cent of the area's exports. The United States pays roughly $4 billion each year for petroleum, coffee, sugar, minerals and a variety of other commodities. Another 30 per cent of Latin America's export trade is with Western Europe. There is relatively little intra-Latin American trade. Few countries of the region carry on more than 10 per cent of their trade with their neighbors. However, they are beginning to pay increasing attention to the possibilities of greater intraregional trade and economic integration. In 1961 the Latin American Free Trade Association (LAFTA) came into being. With the participation of nearly all South American countries, plus Mexico, gains have been registered toward the progressive lowering of tariffs and other barriers to free trade. But under present plans nearly a decade will be needed before truly free trade is achieved. Moreover, LAFTA has not made much headway in the vital fields of integration of industry or in developing agriculture along complementary lines.

Since 1960 a Central American Common Market has been evolving in a relatively satisfactory manner, and in the first four years of its existence commerce among the five member countries more than trebled and is still rising sharply. During this time the combined rate of economic growth has been over 6 per cent yearly.

### Role of Private Foreign Capital

Foreign capital has played a major part in the development of Latin America, but its future role is now a leading political issue in many countries. Prior to 1929 there was a heavy flow of foreign private investment into Latin America. After World War II a renewed stream of capital to the area reached a level of over $750 million a year, until by 1959 direct foreign investment totaled almost $14 billion, three fifths of it from the United States. Private foreign investment in the early 1960's fell off in the wake of the Castro regime's wholesale expropriation of foreign enterprises and an atmosphere of political instability, accompanied by threats of expropriation in several other countries. Indeed, in 1962, earnings repatriated to the United States exceeded the return flow of new private capital, but public funds and loans from international agencies at least partially filled the gap. In recent years, private United States capital has again moved toward the region at a modest rate. But over half of the $350 million annual increase since 1963 is not new external capital; it comes from reinvestment of earnings.

Most of United States private investment in Latin America, which is now valued at $9 billion, is in the extractive fields: 35 per cent in petroleum and 12 per cent in mining, as compared with only 26 per cent in manufacturing, the area which most Latin Americans associate with a major contribution to economic development. Geographical concentration is also great. Thirty per cent of United States investment is in Venezuela; 11 per cent in both Brazil and Mexico; 10 per cent in Argentina; and 9 per cent in Chile.

Widespread Latin American reservations concerning the contribution of private foreign investment reflect deep-rooted feelings that exploitation of nonrenewable resources should be in national hands; that excessive profits are sent home by foreign firms instead of being reinvested; and that foreign capital perpetuates "colonial" economic relationships and works against development and diversification. Many Latin Americans also claim that foreign companies meddle in domestic politics and seek the intervention of their home governments to protect their interests when these clash with the needs of the host country. Relatively few Latin Americans are strongly swayed by arguments that they should pay substantially for the technical know-how of the foreign firms; that profits should be high because of the risks involved or that foreign investment creates new jobs and opportunities for advancement; and that working conditions are better and wages higher in foreign-owned or -controlled companies. Many do, however, recognize that the region lacks the domestic capital to develop its own resources and is vitally dependent upon foreign private capital.

## Background of the Alliance for Progress

The decade of the 1950's witnessed increasing Latin American dissatisfaction with the state of hemispheric economic relations. The end of the Korean war brought a sudden end to artificially high commodity prices to which the economy of the area had become accustomed. Terms of trade deteriorated with a disastrous effect upon efforts at development during a time when the United States was giving most of its foreign aid to Western Europe and Asia. Latin Americans' dissatisfaction over the lack of a positive United States response to their economic aspirations and needs came to a head in 1958. Following an unprecedented outburst of hostility toward the United States, during which Vice President

Nixon was stoned in Caracas, Brazilian President Juscelino Kubitschek proposed a cooperative hemispheric crusade against the evils of underdevelopment. Secretary of State John Foster Dulles' reaction was less than lukewarm. By the time the Eisenhower Administration came forth with a positive program, the Cuban problem had already reached an acute stage, dividing hemispheric opinion and causing new tensions. Thus, the forward steps marked by United States agreement to the establishment of the Inter-American Development Bank (IDB) in 1959 and by our acceptance of the social development goals of the Act of Bogotá in September 1960 lost much of their beneficial impact, being viewed by many Latin Americans as a bribe or an attempted inoculation against *Fidelismo*.

## Birth of the Alliance

Proposing an Alliance for Progress soon after taking office, the Kennedy Administration sought to erect a new edifice of hemispheric cooperation upon the foundation established by the Act of Bogotá. Unfortunately, it was not possible to separate this forward-looking program from the struggle against the Castro regime. The President's proposal came only a month before the Bay of Pigs invasion [by anti-Castro Cubans who were supported by the United States— Ed.], and the shadow of this ill-fated affair lay over the organizing conference in August 1961. Yet the resulting Charter of Punta del Este, which formally brought the Alliance into being, constitutes a very important landmark in hemisphere cooperation. In addition to providing a touchstone for United States programs and policy in the region, it committed the Latin American republics to "a common effort to bring our people accelerated economic progress and broader social justice within the framework of personal dignity and political liberty." It established economic goals in the fields of growth, distribution, diversification and industrialization; set forth comprehensive agrarian reform and universal primary education as top priority social aims; and made maximum domestic self-help a condition for external assistance. The Latin Americans pledged $80 billion over a ten-year period to achieve the goals of the Alliance, while the United States assumed a long-run commitment to insure that external financial assistance would approximate $2 billion annually during this period. Of this, at least half was to come from United States government sources and the rest from international lending institutions, other Western countries and United States private investment.

## Progress of the Alliance

United States government funds obligated as assistance to Latin American countries under the Alliance for Progress have averaged slightly over $1 billion annually since 1961. Programs of the Agency for International Development (AID) constitute some 45 per cent of this amount; other components are Export-Import Bank loans (22 per cent), Food for Peace (18 per cent), and the Social Progress Trust Fund of the IDB (14 per cent). In addition to these direct efforts, the United States has also provided substantial resources to a number of inter-American and other international institutions which furnish large-scale assistance to Latin America's economic and social development. Actual disbursements of external financing, which so far have lagged behind obligations, are now catching up and promise to add measurably to the pace of future development. . . .

What, briefly, are some of the major achievements of the Alliance to date? In material terms substantial results have been obtained. . . . Per capita income rose nearly 5.5 per cent annually in 1964 and 1965 compared with 2.1 per cent in 1963. Latin American countries have mobilized their resources on an impressively large scale, investing well over $30 billion in Alliance-linked projects. Nearly all of them have completed national development plans. In 1961, before the Alliance got under way, only two countries—Mexico and Bolivia—had undertaken major reforms of their land tenure systems. During the ensuing five years a dozen other countries launched programs of agrarian reform in substantial compliance with the commitments undertaken at Punta del Este, Uruguay. The overhaul of tax systems has contributed to a rise of over 25 per cent in tax revenues. Twenty-five million Latin Americans have benefited directly from school lunch and other Food-for-Peace programs. Thousands of classrooms and housing units have been built. Less susceptible to quantification but perhaps of even greater significance has been the completion of basic development studies, the strengthening of development institutions and the growing acccumulation of expertise and skills.

Viewed from another and equally valid perspective, the picture appears far less encouraging. The magnitude of needs is so great that the 30,000 or more classrooms built under Alliance programs have scarcely made a dent on the problem of providing adequate primary school facilities. And while 350,000 housing units have been built, an estimated 20 million are required to provide decent shelter for the urban slum dwellers of Latin America.

Too high a proportion of Alliance funds has gone to meet government budgetary deficits and to bolster efforts to combat acute inflation instead of being committed to development projects or social overhead investments. A large share of export earnings must be used for repayment of, and interest on, the region's heavy external debt. Foreign assistance needs to meet Alliance objectives are estimated at $3 billion for 1966, far above levels thus far achieved. The growth of trade with the United States has slowed markedly during the past year. Self-help efforts have fallen short of objectives, and many reforms to which members of the Alliance are pledged exist more on paper than in reality.

Given the nature of the tasks with which the Alliance has had to contend, it would be surprising if observers did not differ in their assessments of the record of tangible achievements. But when it comes to assessing intangibles, there is much less difference of opinion. Most observers agree that the Alliance has had a negligible impact on the minds of

Latin Americans. It has notably failed to arouse widespread popular enthusiasm. It has generated no political *mystique*. A sense of mass identification, so necessary to the success of a program designed to promote a peaceful revolution by transforming social and economic conditions, is lacking. Thus, despite the real economic gains resulting from the Alliance, it is probably true to say that prevailing attitudes among Latin American masses, as the program reaches the halfway point of its first decade, are characterized more by discouragement and resignation than by hope and optimism.

## THE NEW STATES OF AFRICA [2]

In President Charles de Gaulle's phrase, the newly independent countries of sub-Saharan Africa have achieved "international sovereignty." They are all members of the UN. They all have diplomatic relations with other states. But, in almost every other sense, the task of state-building—that is, of constructing stable governmental structures—awaits them. Indeed . . . they are still confronted with so basic a task as determining the definitive geographic boundaries within which they are to govern.

The Somali Republic, for example, has made claims on all of its neighbors—Ethiopia, Kenya and French Somaliland —to parts of their territories. The Congo (Kinshasa), the Sudan and Nigeria must resolve the problem of whether they will govern within the boundaries established at independence or whether they will split into smaller units. Tanganyika and Zanzibar must decide whether to consummate their present union in the United Republic of Tanzania. The Federation of Mali attempted to build a state within the geographic limits of Senegal and the former French Sudan. However, this federal union burst asunder after nineteen months, and new states are being erected within their former

[2] From pamphlet by Arnold Rivkin, expert on African affairs. (Headline Series no 183) Foreign Policy Association. 345 E. 46th St. New York 10017. Je. '67. p 17-30. Copyright 1967 by Foreign Policy Association, Inc. Reprinted by permission.

geographic limits, with Sudan retaining the name of Mali, while Senegal, for its part, is considering a new type of union with the Gambia to constitute Senegambia.

Thus, it is clear that many African states do not yet have a clear definition of the geographical limits within which they are to exercise their sovereignty. At the same time they are confronted with the problem of the constitutional structure of their governments. Are they to be unitary or federal states? If the former, how centralized or decentralized should they be?

### Nation-Building

Second only to the fundamental problem of state-building is the universal African problem of nation-building. As we have already suggested, the new states south of the Sahara have come to independence with little or no preparation and with little or no sense of national identity. All are confronted with the problem of welding together populations divided by ethnic, tribal, cultural, religious and regional differences. In almost every instance the new states have to create national loyalties which transcend but at the same time are compatible with traditional and local loyalties to tribe, religion and region. For example, a tribe, such as the Ewes, divided between Ghana and Togo, must learn to be Ghanaians and Ewes or Togolese and Ewes. In Mauritania, the Arabic population of the north and the black population of the south must learn to be Mauritanians as well as members of their respective tribes. In the Congo (Kinshasa), a multiplicity of tribes, such as the Bakongo of the western Congo and the Baluba of the south-eastern Congo, which heretofore had very limited contact, must now all learn to be Congolese. . . .

In the larger African countries the problem of fusing together the disparate populations is complicated by vast distances and limited transportation and communication links. In all states, large or small, inadequate or ill-defined governmental structures must relate the outlying parts to the center or capital city. In countries like Ethiopia and Mali, the problem tends, of course, to be aggravated by natural barriers, such as mountains and deserts; in others, such as the Gambia and Malawi, by their odd geographic configurations, and in still others, such as Chad and the Central African Republic, by their isolated, landlocked locations.

Central to the problem of nation-building is the question of the type of political system to be developed to run the government and the degree to which it should be based on persuasion or coercion.

### Trend Toward Authoritarianism

By and large the trend in sub-Saharan Africa has been increasingly toward state-dominated authoritarian political systems involving considerable degrees of coercion. These range from the use of one-party monopolies of power, patronage and means of communication to resort to naked force, e.g., preventive detention, trials by political or military tribunals and confiscation of property. Most African states have, in fact, outright one-party systems or dominant one-party systems in which, as a matter of practice, minority parties are tolerated within narrow limits and only so long as they defer to the will of the dominant party on major issues. In a few instances multiparty systems have attempted, albeit imperfectly, to practice democratic procedures in seeking pluralistic goals. This was the case in pre-coup Nigeria. It also remains the case in the tiny state of the Gambia.

In many of the new countries the political systems have been unable to cope effectively with both the problems of state-building and nation-building and there has been widespread political instability. This has resulted in some twenty military coups d'état and attempted coups since January 1963. For the most part, the military governments, although they have to some degree provided a measure of law and order, have not been very successful in inducing meaningful participation by their people in public affairs.

## *Economy-Building*

Generally speaking, the colonial territories in sub-Saharan Africa have come to independence with dual economies. Most of the new states have relatively small modern sectors in which production is for the market and the exchange of goods is achieved through the use of currency. Most have large subsistence sectors in which production is primarily for home consumption, and such exchange of surplus goods as occurs is unplanned and frequently carried on through barter, with only limited or no use of currency. Thus, every state south of the Sahara is confronted with the need for developing new economic structures. This is sometimes described as extending the market sector or monetizing the subsistence sector. What is required is the development of economic structures involving the conscious production of goods for the market, to be distributed through established marketing channels, with payment in currency or through credits extended by recognized banking institutions.

Characteristically, most of the economic structures in the area have been overwhelmingly concerned with primary production of agricultural and mineral products for the export market. There is a need to diversify production by enlarging the range of primary products produced, by increasing the degree of processing of these commodities and by introducing industrial production on an increasing scale to serve both a growing internal and an external market. . . .

In addition to the basic structural changes involved in economy-building, the new states are confronted with the major decision as to the type of economy they want to build. Should it be an economy with a larger or smaller state-controlled sector? Should it be an economy which encourages private investment, local and foreign, and seeks to develop a significant private sector? Should it be an economy which encourages institutions, such as trade unions, agricultural cooperatives, chambers of commerce and smallholder farmers' groups?

Frequently the new states tend to assign a major role in economy-building to the government and to minimize the role of private entrepreneurs and independent institutions. Part of this trend is an inevitable consequence of the shortage of private entrepreneurs and of capital in the hands of private individuals; of the lack of experience and cultural traditions conducive to economic activity involving production for the market. In part it has grown out of the psychological compulsion, already mentioned, of the new African states to "catch up" with the world's modern affluent states.

In addition, an ideological preference has made itself manifest for a vague but fairly common economic objective frequently called "economic independence" and for an equally vague but fairly common philosophy called "African socialism." The terms are seldom defined and have been employed to describe such sharply contrasting economies as the heavily state-dominated economies of Guinea and Mali, on the one hand, and such relatively open economies as Senegal and Kenya, on the other.

Finally, state-dominated economies with large public sectors have in many ways been an inevitable counterpart of authoritarian one-party states. It would be inherently contradictory to seek to centralize and control all political power, and at the same time encourage and sanction the development of independent economic power outside the reach of the exclusive and aspiring all-powerful one party. The one party inevitably feels the need to avoid competitive or conflicting poles of power, and also the need to control economic units or groups, such as trade unions, cooperatives and trade associations which, although economically motivated, dispose of significant political power. At any rate, this has been the trend. The evolution of Ghanaian one-party authoritarianism before the military coup of 1966 was accompanied by just such an evolution of government combined with party control of the country's economic structure.

## What Kind of Planning?

Experts have been debating how much and what kind of economic-development planning is appropriate for African countries in their present circumstances. Some strongly recommend what has frequently been termed comprehensive planning. This approach seeks to plan for the total economy, the private as well as the public sector—to establish not only planning objectives and goals but also quantitative targets, frequently including production targets. Another school of experts, who are in effect anti-planning "planners," would restrict African planning to identifying a handful of important projects in the public sector. They urge that financing for them be sought within the generally restricted domestic sources available to African countries and from abroad. In between those two extremes there are planners who would seek somehow to impart a sense of order and priority to the use of resources, particularly in the public sector.

Notwithstanding the controversy among the experts, there can be little question that in the circumstances of the sub-Saharan African states, the formulation of a correlated and realistic series of development goals, priorities, policies and approaches is urgently required. There can, for example, be little argument about the need for officials to make a systematic assessment of their country's situation in order to evolve a set of reasonable development goals that are within their capacity to achieve. There can also be little dispute about the need to develop reasonable guidelines for the type of technology, institutions and manpower availabilities (discussed below) each of the new states should seek to develop in its circumstances and in light of its decisions concerning its development goals and policies.

Unfortunately, too many African states have, generally with outside assistance, adopted development plans which have not served their principal needs. Many of the plans have been elaborate exercises which have have been ill-suited and at times irrelevant to the realities of the African states in question. In these instances the plans have been dead letters from the time of their promulgation. . . .

The current status of the economy-building efforts in the area suggests that few of the many basic aspects of the problems have been successfully faced up to. Per capita GNP's [gross national products] ranging from about $40 in Burundi, Malawi and Rwanda to $200-$230 in Ghana, Gabon and Senegal reveal the order of magnitude of the economy-building problem and of the task of "catching-up" with developed countries which have annual per capita GNP's of $2,000 to $3,000.

There have been no dramatic breakthroughs on the economy-building front. The 4 to 5 per cent economic growth rate achieved by Nigeria and the higher rate of the Ivory Coast and Kenya have been among the higher sustained rates achieved in tropical Africa. Most economic growth rates have been less, and in some instances there may have been a post-independence decline in growth. Given the generally assumed population growth rate in the area of 2.5 to 3 per cent, the prevailing economic growth rate suggests that there has been little, if any, actual increase in the annual per capita GNP in most countries in the area, and little, if any, opportunity for the accumulation of domestic capital for productive investment to spur economic growth.

A number of countries have gotten into serious economic and financial difficulties in their postindependence period. Pre-coup Ghana, for example, which had one of the highest per capita GNP's in the area, estimated at $230, and which came to independence with very substantial financial reserves, was brought to the brink of bankruptcy by the overthrown government of Dr. Nkrumah. It dissipated Ghana's resources in nonproductive investment and lavish expenditures. This unfortunate economic performance coincided with a decline in the world market price for cocoa, Ghana's chief export commodity. Mali and Guinea have also, in large part because of misguided ideological policy, had to contend with serious economic maladjustments—inconvertible currencies, shortages of foreign exchange, internal inflation, food and consumer goods shortages, smuggling and illicit currency transactions and mounting unemployment.

## Technological Revolution

Africa's technology ranges from the most modern to the most unbelievably backward equipment and techniques. This is perhaps most strikingly demonstrated in the transportation sector. It is not at all unusual to witness the incongruous sight of a giant jet transport plane, a VC-10 or a Boeing 707, flying overhead and at the same time an African farmer or his wife acting as a beast of burden with a tremendous load of firewood set precariously on his or her back or head, trudging along a crude road hacked out of a rain forest.

In other sectors, although somewhat less striking perhaps, the contrasts are also extreme. In the field of agriculture, it is not uncommon to find, within the short radius of a few miles, Africans operating highly mechanized agricultural equipment, including tractor-driven plows, and still other Africans barely scratching the surface of the earth with pointed digging sticks of the type their ancestors used from time immemorial. In the telecommunications sector one increasingly finds side by side the automated long-distance telephone and the talking drum. In medicine, it is not unusual to find the twentieth century hospital with all of the newest scientific and research equipment and techniques in the capital city and, within fifty miles, the witch doctor still practicing with his fetishes and magic potions, and exorcising evil spirits. And one could cite innumerable other examples, for Africa is caught between the twentieth century technology of the world around it and its own traditional ways of subsistence living.

In short, tropical Africa lacks a graduated ladder of techniques, tools and equipment from which to choose those most suitable to the tasks at hand. It has borrowed without any conscious design or pattern from the technology of the world around it, without particular regard to its own specific circumstances and needs. This is not at all surprising, for there has been little in recent pre- or post-independence African history which would predetermine and shape development of modern technology for production for the market in an orderly way.

However, despite the difficulties, Africa is fortunate to be able to pick and choose and to import much technology already developed and tested from other parts of the world, and it can turn to the outside world for technicians and teachers from whom to receive instruction in the use of the new equipment and methods. Moreover, it has received a reasonable amount of foreign aid, which has enabled it to acquire modern equipment. There has also been, within limits, for those countries seeking it and able and willing to provide sufficient inducements and a friendly welcome, investment from private foreign sources which brings with it not only capital but also modern machinery, techniques, skilled staff and industrial know-how.

What has generally been lacking, however, has been any thought-out concept of the types and levels of technology that the new countries should seek to develop. Frequently governments and their external advisers have failed to appreciate that all imported technology must be adapted to local circumstances and that this requires applied research and experimentation. Too often the importance of scientific research installations for work in applied technology and for training technical personnel has not been recognized. In West Africa, for example, regional research institutions set up by the departed colonial administrations for cocoa cultivation, palm oil production and rice experimentation have, with the first flush of sovereignty, been dismantled or localized to serve only the particular country in which they happened to be physically located. Elsewhere, the absence of immediate visible results has led to neglect in the staffing and financing of national research institutions, and the rush to Africanize such facilities has at times led to the abrupt departure of foreign staff with resultant interruptions and even abandonment of important research efforts.

Also in the absence of thought-through development plans, the quality and levels of imported technology have lacked consistency. Little consideration has been given to the problem of how much and what types of imported technology should be labor-intensive in a continent where generally there is no labor shortage, and how much and what types of imported technology should be capital-intensive in a region where capital is almost always in short supply and, in many instances, scarce. There has frequently been a failure to relate technology in one field to that of closely allied fields. Thus, improved agricultural technology resulting in increased output can be and has, in some instances, already been negated by a failure to improve simultaneously the technology of transportation, storage and marketing of perishable agricultural produce. . . .

### Institution-Building

One of the major problems in elaborating development plans is the institutional gap. Almost everywhere in tropical Africa there is an absence of institutions required to formulate plans and, equally important, to execute them. Most governments lack essential knowledge about the physical features of their countries and do not have the institutions needed to acquire and develop the necessary information and data. Until recently few of the new states had statistical services to provide basic data on the size of their populations or on the amount and value of their production. In these circumstances it is understandably difficult to plan meaningfully a country's food needs or to estimate the amount of investment required to develop educational facilities, health services and the other social services which twentieth century states are committed to provide for their peoples. Similarly, in the absence of necessary production figures, it is difficult, if not impossible, to establish realistic production goals, pro

ject export prospects, and estimate likely public revenue and
foreign-exchange earnings.

## Manpower Development

One of the most vital problems which must be taken into
account in modernizing a country's technology is manpower
development. In the same way that technological development must take place within the framework of a country's
national development plan and within the constraints imposed by an absence of basic institutions, so, too, must it
relate to the state of skilled, trained and experienced manpower in the country. The new states are lacking or seriously
deficient in the skilled manpower necessary for establishing
and sustaining a modern economy. Manpower development
in turn presupposes appropriate training institutions and
national planning goals to accord priorities and establish
targets.

Manpower planning in underdeveloped countries generally is still in its infancy. In sub-Saharan African countries,
either just embarking or only recently embarked upon programs of economic development, there are few guidelines
(and even less hard data) on both manpower requirements
and availabilities. It is necessary in the first instance to make
the best estimates of current needs and availabilities; then,
to make projections based on national planning objectives,
taking into account the country's institutional capacity for
training. Thus, manpower planning has a direct bearing on
size, volume and content of a country's educational effort.
It also has a direct bearing on the establishment of realistic
development objectives or goals for all of the sectors of a
country's economy. It does no good to establish goals for the
expansion of agricultural output if the facilities for training
extension workers, agricultural technicians and marketing
specialists to help achieve the goals cannot conceivably keep
pace with the manpower requirements for attaining the expected rate of increase. Similarly, in the social field it not

only does no good but can actually be harmful to invest large sums in building hospitals and other public health facilities if the prospects for training staff to man them are nonexistent or highly restricted.

There is, therefore, a direct need to phase manpower development planning to institution-building, to development goals and to a country's technological modernization program. Thus, the sub-Saharan states are confronted with multiple sets of major problems which require simultaneous solution if the net result is to be development. Understandably but tragically, all too often, one or another of the problems has been faced, and to some extent successfully; nonetheless the larger development situation has not improved and may actually have deteriorated. For example, construction of school buildings may have proceeded satisfactorily, but the procurement of equipment, preparation of textbooks and teaching materials, and the training of qualified administrative and teaching staff lagged badly, resulting in schools without educational services. Similarly, elsewhere, modern hospital construction proceeded satisfactorily but outstripped by years the training of doctors or nurses and the procurement of equipment and supplies. The result was hospitals without medical services. . . .

In the light of the array of major problems confronting them, it is not surprising that the nascent African states have not as yet made any dramatic breakthroughs to the promised land of political stability and economic development. Increasingly, however, African leaders have begun to recognize the nature of the major problems besetting their countries and have demonstrated a new willingness to approach these problems in a more realistic way. More and more African leaders have also become aware of the need to develop grassroots participation in their countries' political and economic development, of the need to harness local energies, initiatives and resources in coordinated national programs, and of the need for a "revolution from below" in place of the more customary authoritarian one-party-decreed revolutions from above. However, frustration has also developed, as the revolution of rising expectations has outstripped the capacity of the new states to make good on the promises of their political leadership, the hopes engendered by independence and the aspirations nurtured by the many examples of the living standards in the advanced industrial states.

## IMBALANCE IN AFRICA [3]

The total population of Africa is estimated to have been about 325 million in mid-1967 and growing at an annual rate of about 2.5 per cent. More than 40 per cent of the total population of Africa are children under sixteen; about 80 per cent of the adult population are illiterate. With one fourth of the world's land area, Africa only holds 9 per cent of its population. . . . At the same time, while the African population is the least urbanized in the world (with only 13 per cent of the people living in towns of 20,000 or more inhabitants) the rate of urbanization has been more rapid than elsewhere, even more rapid than in Latin America. And among the towns it is the larger ones which have grown fastest, with the towns of 100,000 inhabitants or more gaining population at the rate of 9 per cent per annum. . . .

This relatively small and thinly spread population is furthermore divided into a very large number of tiny sovereign states. Only three countries possess populations of twenty million or more and together they account for over a third of the continent's population. The other 200 million Africans are scattered among thirty-six independent states of whom about thirty have each a total population of less than 5 million. From the point of view of economic management no African country presents problems of excessive size. Besides, the African economies are all as yet relatively simple so that the tasks of planning and of the overseeing of eco-

[3] From *Problems of Plan Implementation: Development Planning and Economic Integration in Africa*, document prepared by United Nations Economic and Social Council. United Nations. New York. '68. p 6-12. Reprinted by permission.

nomic development are potentially rather simple. But at the same time the majority of the African states do not provide an adequate base for integrated national planning. And almost all of them are unable to command enough quantity or concentration of development resources to enable them to make a breakthrough on many of the bottlenecks with which they are faced in the course of plan implementation. . . .

Certain other region-wide data illustrate the typical characteristics of the structures of the African economies. First of all there is the absolute predominance of the agricultural sector in almost every country. Agriculture provides the livelihood for about three quarters of the African population and employs a similar proportion of the labor force. It supplies about 60 per cent of the region's exports and, as far as meaning can be attached to figures in this domain, 30 per cent of the total output of goods and services. At the same time agricultural production has recently stagnated with a growth rate of the order of 1.5 to 2 per cent per annum since 1960. And out of this slow growing total of agricultural supplies, rapidly increasing quantities have had to be exported in order to maintain a modest rate of growth in foreign exchange earnings in the face of unfavorable trends in commodity markets overseas. . . .

The converse of the dominance of the agricultural sector is the smallness of the industrial sector in most African economies. For the region as a whole manufacturing industry makes a contribution to total output which, although it has grown rapidly in recent years as compared to agriculture, still only accounted for less than 12 per cent of Africa's gross domestic product in 1966. . . .

Given the relative weakness of the manufacturing sector, it has been left to the mineral industry and its associated metallurgical enterprises to make the nonagricultural contribution to Africa's foreign trade—about 49 per cent of total exports in 1966. By its very nature, of course, the minerals and metals industry is concentrated in a few countries. Its most dynamic component in recent years has been petroleum where the increase in output has in fact been confined largely to three African countries—Algeria, Libya and Nigeria. The more traditional minerals—copper, iron ore, diamonds, gold, bauxite, manganese phosphates—have been characterized by the usual fluctuations in fortunes arising from changes in production and prices.

But the most important structural characteristic of the mining industries has remained virtually unchanged, namely, their very weak linkage with the rest of the economies in which they are situated, as well as their domination by foreign capital with consequent leakage of the surpluses generated in African mining to other countries. All this, of course, is apart from the fact that this industry is based on a disappearing asset, even though Africa still possesses a considerable proportion of the world's total reserves of various minerals and much of the region has yet to be thoroughly investigated for its resources potential.

The African region is also characterized by a very marked lack of balance between the structure of its production and the structure of its own demand for goods and services. Even counting in the subsistence sector, 25 per cent of the total output of Africa is destined for export markets in order to finance imports on which 22 per cent of all African incomes are spent. Equally striking is the narrowness of the commodity composition of this external trade, especially on the export side. The twenty leading export items already account for more than 70 per cent of African exports while a list of as few as thirty-three items provide almost the entire foreign exchange earnings of the region. And these dominant items are primary products or processed and semiprocessed goods which have to be sold on highly unstable world markets. Though relatively less concentrated, imports into Africa also show the predominance of a small range of items of basic consumption—meat, fish, sugar, cereals, textiles—and intermediate goods such as mineral fuels.

The concentration in the direction of Africa's external trade is equally striking. Despite some recent diversification of trading contacts, notably in the direction of increased trade with the Socialist countries, Africa still does the overwhelming bulk of its trading with a few advanced countries in Western Europe—67 per cent of all exports and 54 per cent of imports in 1966.

The high concentration in both direction and composition of Africa's external trade, coupled with the very large share of external trade in total economic activity in the region has made this a source of considerable economic insecurity and consequently one of the major obstacles to well-based planning and to the smooth implementation of development plans. The stage has been reached in many countries where the relative merits of employing additional resources in producing for export as against producing for local consumption have to be weighed with some care, making due allowance for the value of greater economic security and independence. Some rethinking of national food policies has already started in some countries. And the increasing difficulties arising from high foreign trade dependence also makes more pressing the task of carrying through measures of economic integration so as to allow of realistic import substitution in certain branches.

## The Adoption of Planning in Africa

Largely following the movement of thought and practice in the metropolitan countries of Europe and sometimes under the direct guidance of those governments, many of the colonial administrations in Africa were already experimenting with development planning, usually at a very elementary level of sophistication, before the big era of African independence set in. . . .

In some African countries a deliberate choice of methodology has been made at the time of the introduction of planning, taking into account the existing supply of statistical material and other relevant factors. However, the more usual situation is that the approaches and the methods of planning that have been used in the colonial period and carried over into the period of independence have been those that were familiar to the metropolitan powers. For the future, there would seem to be need for a more deliberate choice of planning methods in each case taking into account particularly the statistical and manpower situation which is generally relatively underdeveloped in the African countries. . . .

The social and institutional framework within which planning was introduced into Africa was also relatively unhostile. In important questions such as land tenure and taxation, conditions in Africa have been relatively favorable to planning and change. The low population densities for a while protected the colonial and postcolonial African governments from the sort of overwhelming need for radical social reforms under which planning has had to be carried out in some other regions from the very initial stages. From an administrative point of view most African countries are small entities into which planning could be introduced without raising the sort of unmanageable organizational problems that have arisen in some other regions.

The familiarity of African governments and administrations with planning concepts and processes has not by itself been able to assure a uniformly close adherence to national development plans. In particular, many of the modifications . . . of government policies that are required to facilitate the successful implementation of the development plans have not been made. In all too many cases when sudden contingencies, especially those arising from foreign trade and external financial assistance, have occurred the first victim to be sacrificed has been the plan. There are too few instances where African governments have been able to insulate the course of planned development to any reasonable degree from internal and external events. There are also too many instances where the government's ability to implement its own development plan has been undermined by other aspects of its own policies particularly those relating to domestic political affairs and external relations.

Many African governments seem to have been unprepared for the sudden realization that national development, especially planned development aiming at maximum growth and important structural transformation, is a very slow process. The capacity to persevere over a period of time in carrying out a coherent program of development is one of the necessary requirements for successful plan implementation which has to be deliberately cultivated by the governments themselves. A very important contributory factor in the failure of many governments to persist in the implementation of their development plans is the frequency with which plan forecasts turn out to diverge from the actual course of events. It is difficult for the political leaders, the civil servants and the population at large to appreciate that a plan can still have validity as a guide to action even though its specific quantitative predictions are not exactly realized.

The majority of African governments have not taken enough steps to improve their own chances of successfully implementing their development plans by carrying out the minimum necessary measures of administrative reform. While the existing systems of administration may not be in most cases positively hostile to planning, that by itself is not sufficient to assure successful implementation plans. Conscious, and often far-reaching, reforms of the machinery of government are needed in order to assure that the people and the various institutions on whose efficient performance successful plan implementation depends will understand what they are supposed to be contributing and will have the means, within the day-to-day organization of their work, to carry out the tasks expected of them.

## INDESIA: POOR PEOPLE IN A RICH LAND [4]

Travel the islands of Indonesia—an equatorial nation that is one of the world's largest and most populous—and you find

[4] From article in *U.S. News & World Report*. 63:50-4. D. 25, '67. Reprinted from *U.S. News & World Report*.

the constant contrast of a poor people living in a rich land ... :

Per capita income of $65 a year in a country with the Far East's largest petroleum reserves;

Malnutrition, even occasional starvation, in a land that could feed other nations in addition to itself;

A threatened social breakdown among a people with an extraordinary sense of community effort.

But it is out in the rural villages and small towns, where 4 of every 5 Indonesians live, that the contrasts of poverty and great potential wealth take on real meaning.

In the West Sumatra town of Padangsidempuan, for example, nightfall means going through dim streets lighted only by kerosene lamps and candles. Yet close to the town are half a dozen potential sites for hydroelectric projects.

Local residents don't even speculate about a power dam. They would be happy with just a road they could use for hauling crops to a nearby port. There was a good highway twenty-five years ago, but mile after mile of it has washed away, down to bedrock.

Indonesia's natural resources are among the world's richest: oil, rubber, tin, bauxite, iron ore, nickel and other minerals. A rich volcanic soil will grow almost anything suited to a tropical climate. . . .

Present-day Indonesia and its people provide some signposts to the future of this rich, restless nation.

Just as there is no truly "typical American," there is no "average Indonesian"—not in a country with ten major languages and at least sixty different dialects; nine distinct ethnic groups; four religions, and barely two decades of national independence.

But some things are common to representative Indonesians. Such an Indonesian is small, wiry, brown-skinned, but more Polynesian than Oriental in appearance. He is likely to be a peasant farmer, living on the same land his family has tilled for generations. He is artistic, polite, gentle

—except for occasional outbursts of individual or mass savagery—and feels hungry if he can't eat rice every day.

This Indonesian's thoughts and actions are governed much more by community traditions than by statute law. He is deeply though not formally religious, and very much a mystic, whether he calls himself a Moslem, Hindu or Christian. He has very sharp prejudices against Chinese people. And, over the past generation, he has learned to live with inflation, deal with corruption and survive amid national chaos.

### Land of Three Thousand Islands

Indonesia is a 3,300-mile-long chain of nearly three thousand islands. Many are mere dots on the sea—an acre or less of palm trees and sand even at low tide. But some others —Sumatra, Borneo and the Indonesian half of New Guinea, or West Irian—are among the world's largest islands. In all, the country's land area covers 735,000 square miles, about one fourth the size of the United States.

Indonesia's 110 million people make it the world's fifth most populous nation. But the population is very unevenly divided. More than 70 per cent is on one island, Java, where as many as two thousand people sometimes try to grind out a living on one square mile of land. The phrase "teeming masses" takes on real meaning along a Javanese highway at sundown as literally thousands of people, walking side by side or riding bicycles, leave no room for automobiles.

At the other extreme are the empty interiors of Borneo —now officially called Kalimantan—and Sumatra, where you can drive for an hour without meeting another car or seeing more than half a dozen people along the rutted, boulder-strewn route that passes for a highway.

To the eye, Indonesia looks like anything from a South Sea paradise to a squalid urban slum to an Alpine village. There are terraced rice fields, jagged mountain peaks, dashing mountain streams flowing into sluggish coastal swamps, more than seven hundred volcanoes, tangled vines that form a truly impenetrable jungle, and neat farms marked out in mathematical precision. Lowland climate is hot and steamy, but in the mountains—some of them more than a mile and a half high—heavy sweaters and blankets are welcome.

Transportation is a nightmare. From the tip of Sumatra to West Irian's border with Australian Papua is farther than from New York to San Francisco. Only one island, Java, has an all-weather road linking its main cities. Just two islands, Java and Bali, are connected by regular ferries. Air service is haphazard at best. . . .

In many ways, the country is more an accident of history than a natural geographic or economic unit. A traveler quickly discovers sharp differences among the major islands and their people.

The most noticeable variances are between Java and the rest of the nation. These are reflected in the common Javanese reference to any other part of Indonesia as "the other islands." Java is political Indonesia, the island of officials and army officers. Javanese delight in maneuver and deviousness, in talk for the sake of talk.

Sumatra, about the size of California, is the treasure-chest island. It accounts for about 70 per cent of the entire export revenue of the country. Sumatrans tend to be less formal, more adventurous, than other Indonesians.

People from Sulawesi—formerly Celebes—are quick to explain that they are more "Western" in outlook, more aggressive and systematic in their thinking. Balinese keep to a life apart, centered on religious rituals and elaborate ceremonies, while most of the people of West Irian are barely out of the Stone Age.

If any one thing shapes and symbolizes Indonesia, it is rice. Political arguments and inflation indexes revolve around the price of rice. Economic plans hinge on rice production. The requirements for growing the irrigated rice—the constant cooperation among neighbors in sharing water, planting and harvesting—spawned villagers' communal approach to life. Indonesians seldom do anything by themselves. Just as they work the fields together, they repair roads, clean irrigation ditches—even go to market together.

Rice, however, means more than just calories. Feed an Indonesian a Western dinner, complete from onion soup through sirloin steak to pie and ice cream, and he still complains that he hasn't been given rice.

Rice growing is largely manual labor, although oxen and water buffalo are used to pull iron-tipped wooden plows and harrows across flooded fields. Planting, weeding and harvesting are all done by hand.

In most places, rice is threshed by treading the heads underfoot, and prepared for use by pounding with an oversized mortar and pestle.

Throughout Indonesia, in fact, a basic source of power is a man's or an animal's muscles. From sunrise until nightfall, Indonesian roads carry a steady stream of men bearing heavy loads balanced on shoulder poles, or slow-moving oxcarts piled high with timber, coconuts and other goods. The commonest taxi is a horse-drawn cart or the ever-present *betjak*, a pedicab on three bicycle wheels by which it would be possible, if one had the patience, to travel the 650-mile length of Java.

Very few Indonesians are industrial workers. It is estimated that, in the entire country, there are only about three hundred factories with more than one hundred employees each. There was no industry at all until the 1930's, and it still is limited mainly to food processing, textiles and other consumer goods.

Only about 6 per cent of the people earn their living from industry, compared with more than 70 per cent from agriculture. The latter includes the millions working full or part time on the rubber, tea, coconut and other plantations whose products make up the biggest part of Indonesia's exports.

Well over half of all families work at some kind of "cottage industry" at home, partly for a small added income and partly because there is nothing else to do. Even rice farming, with its great labor requirements, cannot keep people busy all the time.

Most Indonesians, particularly in Java, are natural crafts- men. Women work hour after hour on the intricately de- signed and dyed batik cloth that is the basis of the national dress. Men carve wood, work silver and make cigarettes. Whole families weave cloth and make reed baskets. Paper is scarce despite immense pulpwood resources, so in most stores purchases are put into loosely woven baskets instead of paper bags.

Even with all this, it is estimated that 3 million Indo- nesians are jobless and another 15 million seriously under- employed. In any village you see scores of men sitting idle hour after hour—talking, drinking tea or holding gamecocks. Partly, this is cultural; Indonesian family life is oriented toward giving men leisure for such things. More than that, however, it is a simple lack of work.

Land for farming is limited. The average family land- holding in Java is less than two acres, barely enough for sub- sistence farming. For all his work, the average Indonesian is not a productive farmer. He badly needs more fertilizer and credit and better tools and techniques, but he cannot afford any of these. Most farmers, explains an agricultural adviser, are simply too poor to take risks with new ideas.

An Indonesian's first loyalty is to his family, and the fam- ily embraces a long list of distant cousins and in-laws whom the Western world hardly considers relatives. This provides great social stability and an automatic system for caring for the aged, infirm and jobless. It also breeds wide-ranging nep- otism. Government agencies and company offices are crowded with people whose only job qualification is being someone's cousin. But few criticize or question the system.

## A Look at Religions

About 90 per cent of all Indonesians are considered Moslems, but many cheerfully admit that they are only "statistical" Moslems. Even on Fridays, the Islamic Sabbath, most mosques are only sparsely attended.

The basic religion of Indonesia—and one of the most fundamental forces in the country—is centuries-old mystic animism, with various Hindu, Buddhist and Islamic ideas tacked on.

The core of this religion is maintaining harmony with natural forces, supernatural forces and one's fellow man. Throughout Java, for example, and on many other islands, every stalk of rice is cut in a certain way, with a tiny knife concealed in the palm of the hand, so as not to offend the rice goddess, Devi Sri.

Islamic belief is strong enough, however, to stymie badly needed birth-control measures, especially in rural areas where population pressures are most acute. Easy divorces, possible for men under Islamic law, make many women eager for large families. If a woman is divorced, it is the children who are supposed to support her.

Still, population limitation is winning favor. Many Indonesian women practice rudimentary forms of birth control, or eat supposedly abortive herbs and roots. A sure sign of demand for contraceptive devices is the sale of intrauterine loops in urban black markets for $10 or more each, an enormous price by local standards. . . .

For more than a generation, Indonesians have learned to exist alongside inflation and near breakdown of the economic order. The country's inflation is among the most severe of modern times. Prices rose 700 per cent in 1965, and 1,500 per cent in the hectic 12 months before July 1966. Despite drastic austerity measures imposed by the new government, monthly price jumps of 3 to 5 per cent are common.

Many people are spared the direct blast of inflation. These are the rural dwellers living mostly by subsistence farming and bartering for as much as they buy with cash.

Hardest hit are city wage earners, particularly the white-collar workers. "Hyperinflation makes cash wages meaningless. The great lure of a government job is not the salary of a few dollars a month, but the "rice ration" is furnished to each worker.

Many private employers also are required by law or union contract to provide each worker with a rice ration, which includes enough grain to sustain a family, some cloth, cooking oil and other essential commodities. The great goal of city dwellers is to hold two jobs, preferably a government post with its rice ration, and a second job for cash income.

Hyperinflation is a root cause of Indonesia's widespread corruption. The middle-level bureaucrat is caught in a grim dilemma. He earns the equivalent of $15 a month. The white shirt he must wear to work costs $2 or $3. The bicycle he rides to the office costs at least $25. So, to feed and clothe his family, he takes cash bribes or cartons of cigarettes—which he later sells on the black market—in return for his signature or stamp on one of the countless documents required for the simplest transaction.

Similarly, smuggling of copra and other commodities to Singapore by military commanders is regarded as morally bad, and it diverts revenue from the national treasury. But, in addition to lining a few pockets, it provides cash to feed and house troops who otherwise would probably mutiny.

At the start of . . . [1967], Indonesia was as near physical paralysis as a theoretically modern nation could be. Engineers say a massive highway-repair effort in Java saved the road network from actual collapse by only a few months. Many of Sumatra's roads are completely gone.

Poor transportation is one reason there is often hunger in a fertile land. In 1966, more than ten thousand people starved on one side of the island of Lombrok, although there was ample rice only fifty miles away. Rice prices sometimes vary tremendously within a radius of a few miles because of poor, expensive transportation.

There is still too much natural food available for famine to be a major danger. Yet there is widespread malnutrition. Doctors say protein and other diet deficiencies make millions of people far less healthy than they look. . . .

## Indonesia's Racial Problem

Like the United States, Indonesia is a multiracial society that glorifies tolerance but has a severe race problem. Here it is the Chinese who are the targets of prejudice. Unlike United States Negroes, the Chinese are near the top of the economic ladder.

The reasons for this, and for the whole race problem, go back many decades. As the Dutch tightened their control over the country, they frequently used Chinese as their local agents, overseers and tax collectors. Thus the Chinese became identified with foreign "oppression."

The Chinese also traditionally worked harder, saved more and took greater risks than Indonesians. Though Chinese are only 3 per cent of the population, some observers believe they control one third of all private business.

Few years pass without anti-Chinese rioting somewhere in the country. April riots in the city of Semarang injured dozens and left scores of Chinese homeless.

As far back as 1959, decrees barred Chinese from various professions and from doing retail or wholesale business in smaller towns. In central Java, "foreigners," meaning Chinese, were required to paint their names in red letters on shops and homes. The aim was to drive the Chinese to the cities and ultimately out of the country.

The Chinese are still in Indonesia, probably because the Sukarno government's enforcement of the anti-Chinese laws was as erratic and inept as almost everything else it did. Now, official policy is assimilation; Chinese are urged to adopt Indonesian names and citizenship.

At best, any assimilation will take generations, because feelings run so deep. A student leader at the university in Bandung, for example, describes himself as a "moderate" on the Chinese question: He thinks it is right to bar Chinese from various businesses and professions simply because of their race, but "it is wrong to burn down their houses."

Though much of Indonesia has not changed for generations, change appears to be coming soon. Increased literacy and cheap transistor radios bring ideas from a world that until now existed only dimly for most villagers. Better roads mean more markets and more income. They also create wants that soon become necessities.

Such new social tensions, added to the race friction, are disrupting a once-placid life. Indonesia's society of villages that are almost a world to themselves is increasingly unable to cope with population pressures and other midcentury problems. But, so far, nothing else has come along for the poor people in a rich land.

## CAN INDIA SURVIVE CALCUTTA [5]

June is a bad month for Calcutta. The heat lies heavily on the city like a foul-smelling blanket; decay seems to spread before your eyes. There are more flies, garbage, anger, cholera and death than in the other seasons but even less will to think about them. In the white glare of the tropical sun Calcutta is harder than ever on the gorge. The choking sensation comes earlier and you retreat: The tourist boards the next plane; the businessman sends his family to a resort in the Himalayan foothills and ensconces himself in the shadiest, coolest corner of his club; would-be writers and politicians pass long hours gossiping under the fans of coffeehouses; laborers crouch on pavements thirstily gulping watery milk from green coconuts. Those with no retreat, not even the price of a coconut, try to sleep off, or at least sleep through, their hunger, exhaustion and despair.

But it is even worse in July when the monsoon blows off the Bay of Bengal, especially for the million or more persons who live in the unimproved mud hovels called *bustees* and the hundred thousand or so who live on the sidewalks. Then the decades of neglect that have made India's largest, most

⁵ From article by Joseph Lelyveld, correspondent. New York *Times Magazine.* p 58-60+. O. 13, '68. © 1968 by The New York Times Company. Reprinted by permission.

vital and culturally alert city the world's worst urban disaster are impossible to ignore.

In those sections where they exist at all, ancient sewers clog and overflow, turning whole streets into filthy, fetid canals. The *bustee* areas, which boast what may well be the worst urban density statistics known anywhere, become hopeless swamps. Any narrow lane in Calcutta's *bustees* in the monsoon season could make the River Styx look like a crystal mountain stream.

Calcutta is not one disaster but many, each breeding its own kind of despair, its own special nightmare. The city planner scans the decaying water, sanitation and transport systems and holds out the prospect of total failure, a breakdown so complete that people would flee as if running from war or plague. The sociologist talks of the frayed fabric of society coming apart altogether, the economist of a depression so deep there could never be any recovery. The political analyst resorts to words like "anarchy" and "nihilism" and asks whether Indian democracy can survive the erosion of faith that is taking place here.

These nightmares seem an inescapable part of the future demographers see for Calcutta. Twenty years from now, they say, there will be 12 million people living in the metropolitan area, as against 7.5 million in the stifling conditions of today. But the unthinkable is not just in the future; it is here and now. Calcutta is already the worst example of a malignancy of social purpose, organization and resources that can be found in a number of cities in the world's poorest countries (not to mention some that are not so poor). There is no relief in the fact that it has professional and entrepreneurial skills, political and literary sophistication that would be hard to match in any city in a remotely comparable predicament. That simply raises the question: Why haven't these good, earnest people made more of a difference?

Maybe Calcutta never had a chance. The city has been dying ever since it was founded 280 years ago by British merchants so eager to expand their trade with India's rich heartland that they established themselves in the midst of a malarial swamp. A century later that swamp was the capital of British India, remaining "the second city" of the Empire —after London—till the Viceroy packed off to Delhi fifty-six years ago.

Even today—when the old British mansions have rotted like vegetables, their neo-Grecian facades turned green with mold, their insides converted into dense, dank warrens for the dispossessed—there is no place in India where the well-off, Indian or foreign, live more spaciously. A family of four may not expect to retain 110 servants as some of the British nabobs did in the eighteenth century when Calcutta was divided between a "white town" and a "black town." But the clubs are as well secluded from the turmoil of the streets as they ever were; the swimming, polo, golf, tennis and horse racing haven't declined at all. . . .

The breath-taking contrasts between luxury and squalor may stun the newcomer, but then they always have. . . .

The proof is in the grisly stare of vultures hunched ominously on apartment house rooftops at the edge of the city. Or it is, quite simply, in the fact of starvation deaths. The Indian government doesn't like to concede that there's starvation in the country, and so splits hairs by insisting that all grossly undernourished persons who die are actually carried off by identifiable diseases—thereby sidestepping the fact that it is precisely the lack of food that makes killers of what would otherwise be curable ailments.

Considering that the government has managed to avoid outright famine in the twenty-one years of independence, its sensitivity is at least understandable. But a habit of not seeing distasteful facts has more to do generally with callousness than sensitivity, especially in Calcutta where someone dies of hunger every day.

One evening I saw a beggar woman of indeterminate age drop dead in the middle of a milling crowd on Chowringhee, the busy main thoroughfare. (Most of the very poor in Calcutta are too ravaged to reflect the distinctions of the years.

Young and old, they are equally wasted.) At first no one stopped to regard her rigid remains; prone bodies on sidewalks aren't, after all, very rare here. Then a meticulous middle-class woman in a fresh white sari happened to look down and halted, confused. I went to look for help and found a traffic policeman. "Was it a traffic accident?" he asked after I conveyed the information that a woman was lying dead on the pavement nearby. Told no, the policeman shrugged and turned his back. I turned away, too.

In Calcutta you learn to avert your eyes from squalor, then not to see it at all. The outsider starts by being appalled by the professional beggars who pursue him on his walks—the paralytics moving like reptiles, the lepers with deformities so hideous they can hardly be believed, the naked boys whining, "No mama, no papa; Sahib, baksheesh." Then he hates them for being so downcast. Finally he is able to ignore them totally or, what may be worse, to respond with that absent-minded philanthropy of some Indians who can be seen complacently dropping a coin in a beggar's hand without registering any awareness of his existence other than as an object of their charity.

The outsider may even come to appreciate the skill of some of the con men he meets—the bright-eyed Sikh who hustles up to pin a paper Indian flag to his shirt and demand support for some unnamed patriotic cause; the well-spoken, desperate-looking Anglo-Indian who explains in English that he is a soldier in need of bus fare to return to his base. When you tell him, "That's what you said last week," he is unruffled. "Oh, so we've met," he replies. "Well, give me a rupee anyway for old time's sake."

The con men and professional beggars—of whom there are said to be a small army of 5,000 or 6,000, often deployed in gangs—are but the most startling and visible of vast legions that have no hope of regular employment and so, to survive, must invent livelihoods for themselves out of nothing. There is no place on earth where more people work so hard doing so little that is necessary or productive. Calcutta has more hawkers (or so one soon imagines) than most cities have people, each straining every day to sell one or two fountain pens, a pair of sunglasses, some old clothes, toys made out of tin cans—anything that will earn a rupee or two to keep going.

They are always desperate and sometimes their wares reflect a desperate, almost antic ingenuity. One hawker on Chowringhee peddles silhouettes of a jungle scene of elephants and palm trees he has managed to carve out of old 78 rpm records, with the label of His Master's Voice in the center as a setting sun. I bought one that had been fashioned from the second movement of the Second Brandenburg Concerto with Leopold Stokowski conducting the Philadelphia Symphony Orchestra. . . .

Or there are those who deal in waste materials like coal dust and cow dung. Coal dust can be mixed with mud to produce a fuel called *gool,* which can then be bartered or sold in the form of patties. This is the poor people's fuel. Bepin Tikadar, who is sixty-five, and his twenty-nine-year-old son, Ratan, manufacture patties of cow dung and sawdust, which is regarded as a higher-grade mixture. They have lived for more than twenty years in the Panchanantala Road *bustee* area, which is, to be precise, one hell of a place—a narrow wedge of a couple of acres on the shoulder of a suburban rail line in which five thousand persons are squeezed together. Just across the road the government is building tall apartment houses for civil servants, who have to keep their curtains drawn if they don't want to see the *bustees* or the young children wandering out on the tracks where, every now and then, one of them fails to get out of the way of an onrushing express.

The Tikadars pay the man who owns a cowshed nearby two rupees a month per cow for all the dung his herd produces and a sawmill one rupee for every gunny sack of sawdust they use. One hundred patties made from this mixture sell for thirty-six paise, about 4.5 cents. None of their neighbors in the *bustee* area can afford to buy the fuel, even at that low price, so they have to solicit customers in other, more comfortable neighborhoods. The firm of Tikadar & Son nets about four rupees a day, the income on which the eight members of the family have to subsist.

Like most of Calcutta's poor, the Tikadars have never really been assimilated into the life of the city. Their *bustee* area is more like a village—one whose fields have been devoured by locusts—than a typical urban slum. Asked why he doesn't seek training for some industrial skill, Ratan Tikadar shrugs his knobby shoulders and replies, "How can I? Who'd feed my family while I was being trained?"

And yet he is comparatively lucky. Not everyone can invent a livelihood as secure as his. In the bottomless lower depths of Calcutta there must be several hundred thousand additional labor seekers who have no regular jobs and nothing to offer but their overstrained, undernourished bodies. Here men compete with cattle for labor, leaving the spavined, neglected animals to wander free in the streets, further snarling the traffic.

As you ride into the city from the airport on the desolate strip of cracked asphalt known as the Dum Dum Superhighway, you see men on the banks of the canals hauling barges piled high with jute, like mules. As you turn into the crowded streets, you find them pulling and shoving carts laden with anything from iron rods and bricks to coal or foodstuffs, doing work only a bullock would do in most other Indian cities. Everywhere there are the ricksha wallahs, expatriates from the overcrowded villages of the Gangeatic plain, who pad barefoot on the broiling hot pavement through the melting tar by day and sleep in colonies on the sidewalks by night so they can send home the equivalent of $3 or $4 a month. In this way, something like $40 million are sent out of Calcutta to the countryside every year in the form of pitiably small postal remittances.

More staggering in its way than the squalor of Calcutta is its dislocation. The city is a great machine whose gears always grind, never mesh. Obviously there is no shortage of the manpower required to build new schools, lay new streets, dig the ditches for the missing water mains and sewers, or simply clear away the great mounds of garbage that accumulate in the streets. What is missing is the ability to relate the effort to the need.

The missing ability to relate seems even more basic to the city's predicament than any missing funds. It's easy to list Calcutta's problems and their manifold causes, harder but still not very hard to rattle off possible solutions. What is really difficult is to understand why all the listing and rattling have remained just that while conditions daily grew more intolerable. Greed and complacency have played their part, but worst of all has been the paralysis of resignation. . . .

Businessmen complain constantly of the low productivity that results from chronic labor unrest. But they are non-plussed when asked what could be done in Calcutta. An engineer whose firm has done sophisticated "feasibility studies" on development projects from Kenya to Korea can think of nothing more feasible than a campaign to persuade shop-keepers to clean the pavements in front of their shops.

Radical Bengali intellectuals, who make this the only Indian city that one could even think of calling cosmopolitan, seem almost permanently out of phase. Nowhere in India is there more social consciousness, but nowhere does it seem so unfocused on its surroundings. Confronted with an overwhelming urban catastrophe, the intellectuals debate Maoist formulas for agrarian revolt. Understandably that seems easier than coming to terms with the city. . . .

An outsider is hard put to decide whether the desperate state of Calcutta is a reflection of all that is romantic and despairing in the Bengali mind, or whether the often desperate state of the Bengali mind is a reflection of Calcutta. Bengalis tend to blame conditions in their city on everyone but themselves—unfeeling officials in New Delhi, Hindi-speaking refugees from the Ganges basin, who make up an increasingly large portion of its population, Western businessmen with their eyes only on their profit margins, or

Mewari speculators from the deserts of Rajasthan in western India, who have put very little back into Calcutta for the fortunes they have made here.

Most of their grievances are unshakably real. The partition of India twenty-one years ago flooded the city with refugees from East Pakistan while depriving it of the greater part of its hinterland. Calcutta may still be India's largest city, her most important manufacturing center and port, but the truncated state of West Bengal is one of the smallest in the Indian union and, therefore, easy to ignore. Sixty years ago it was said: "What Bengal thinks today, India will think tomorrow." But now that rings hollow.

Indeed, if Bengal is to be a model again for the rest of India, it could only be by becoming a graveyard for the democratic institutions Bengalis helped to create. Nursing their grievances, almost seeming to cherish them, Bengalis have gotten used to a violent and disruptive style of politics that sometimes seems to have no ideology other than masochism. Last year the Congress party was voted out of power for the first time since independence and replaced by a loose absurdity of a coalition with fourteen (count them!) constituent parties, the strongest of which were Communist. . . .

The real question is not whether the Communists will win the coming election, though they might; it is whether any stable and effective government can ever be elected here again. At present that hardly seems likely. Already the civil servants who have been serving as caretakers in the state since the collapse of the last government of politicians are telling themselves they can run Calcutta better than the party hacks. Considering that none of the parties—left, right or center—has shown anything deeper than an oral commitment to doing something to arrest the festering of Calcutta, they may have a point. But if democracy is to be written off here, its devaluation elsewhere in the country could only be a matter of time. And even then the last word would not have been said, for whoever took over India would still have to cope with Calcutta.

Meantime, it is pointless today to look for even an oral commitment from the civil service on rescuing the city. The service's job is simply to keep it from becoming a greater nuisance than it is. "If you can keep order on the streets from seven in the morning till nine at night," a member of the establishment said, defining the role of government here, "you've done everything that can be expected."

The deadly resignation about Calcutta that the politicians seem to share with the intellectuals and businessmen was reflected last year when the Calcutta Metropolitan Planning Organization, a body of professional optimists, presented a carefully drawn master plan for saving and developing the city. Not many people in Calcutta thought the plan had a chance of ever being implemented. One commentator went so far as to dismiss it as "a cruel and unseemly joke." This reaction may have said something for Calcutta's sophistication, but it also meant there was no substantial body of local opinion lending its active support to the plan. While the politicians in New Delhi pondered how to parcel out the nation's scanty resources, nobody was standing up for Calcutta.

The city's planners, who were guided by a team of Ford Foundation experts, calculated that more than $25 million a year would be needed in the plan's first five years. They were promised only half that by the central government—only to receive less than half of what they were promised.

These promises are now being revived. The new Indian Five-Year Plan that is in the process of being drafted is said to aim at an expenditure of 720 million rupees (about $96 million) here. That amount won't begin to meet the need, but the planners are convinced that a larger sum would be squandered. They have a point. The crisis of Calcutta not only has yet to become a national priority; it has yet to become a high priority in Calcutta itself: the city has the highest land values and lowest property taxes in India.

The first task the planners set is to halt the runaway deterioration of every public facility and save the port, which is silting up. They despair of getting rid of the *bustees* in this century but argue that these hovels could be made fit for habitation if they were provided with safe drinking water, underground sewerage and electric lighting. That would require taking the land on which they stand away from the real-estate speculators who now own it, something probably that only a strong Communist government in the state would be ready to do. . . .

The planners talk, too, about a second bridge over the Hooghly River and, more theoretically, about a mass transit system. They even discuss the rationalization of the Calcutta area's administration, which is incoherently parceled out to thirty-five separate governing bodies, all essentially predatory.

A group of American and British urban experts came to Calcutta to study the city and plan. They concluded they had "not seen human degradation on a comparable scale in any other city in the world." The plan, they said, was "a realistic and humane statement of the minimum action required to avert a final breakdown." Nearly two years later, the plan remained on the shelf. The "minimum," it seemed, was too much.

But then it is easy to understand why pronouncements about a "final breakdown" fail to jolt anyone into action in Calcutta, for it takes a cruel and restless imagination to grasp the concept of a breakdown any more final than the one with which the city is already confronted.

Since independence, barely five miles of major new roadway have been added to relieve the congestion of the streets. The proposals for a mass transit system have been under discussion for nearly twenty years with absolutely no result. Meantime at least one third of the city's buses and trams can be relied upon to be out of service at any given time. It is remarkable that any ever work, for almost nothing is done about maintenance and absolutely nothing about the replacement of aged vehicles that normally carry twice their

prescribed passenger loads, with the more daring of the surplus passengers getting little more than a foot or hand inside.

Transportation being so near to hopeless, little can be
done to relieve the overcrowding of the center of the city
where approximately one third of the population lives in
*bustees,* and considerably more than half in conditions of
extreme urban squalor. In any case, the very poor in Calcutta are too poor to ride the trams. Obviously, then, the
relevance of the new public housing on the outskirts of the
city to the problem of the *bustees* is zero—minus zero, in fact,
for it falls short by thirty thousand units a year of what
would be required to keep pace with the rate of population
growth.

The simplest way to describe conditions of sanitation in
the *bustees* is to say there aren't any. Narrow lanes, often no
more than a couple of yards wide, are half given over to
open drains whose moldering, putrefying contents run past
every doorstep. In the grimmest of the hovels a fully grown
man can neither stand nor lie at his full length, but families
of five or six can be found jammed together on the damp
earth floors. Only in the best *bustees* are there solid walls
between one such—apartment? domicile? pen? stall?—and the
next. Usually there are just a few boards, a strip of corru-
gated iron or a curtain fashioned from an old gunny sack.
Having seen the *bustees,* the visitor revises his snap judgment that the pavement dwellers must be the worst-off people in the world.

To the squeamish onlooker, Calcutta's very poor are so
depressed that they do not seem quite human. The question
is always posed—*How can human beings live like that?*—as
if they did so by choice. When the choice is between a *bustee*
and a pavement, the answer is not so obvious, especially if
all of one's friends live on the pavement. It is striking how
often the lives of the pavement dwellers reflect conventional
virtues of stability, order and even cleanliness. Many bathe
twice a day. If they do so standing in the gutter at the communal tap, that is only because there is no other place.

They rent a mail box, instead of a room, so they can have the address they need to qualify for a ration card, and sleep on the same patch of pavement every night in the midst of the same people, their community. It is even possible to find families that have lived on the pavements for several generations. Of course there are also drifters—not as many as might be expected but more than enough, for among them are packs of young boys.

With the incredible congestion, garbage collection should be daily at least. The problem is complicated by the need to remove human wastes from more than forty thousand fly-breeding open privies. But two thirds of the city's sanitation trucks are normally out of commission, so collection is weekly, bimonthly or virtually unknown. To make matters worse, while New York last year was paralyzed by one garbage strike, Calcutta had thirty-five.

Each crisis opens onto another. With offal everywhere and the ancient pipes rotting, little can be done to insure the purity of the drinking water. The water system was excellent—in the last century; now, however, two thirds of Calcutta's water comes unfiltered direct from the polluted Hooghly River. Only in recent years has the unfiltered water been chemically treated to reduce the constant menace of epidemic cholera, but it still is a sure source of a whole catalogue of other gastrointestinal infections. . . .

The neglect of the educational system is even more alarming. Since independence, the only new public-school buildings erected in the city have replaced dilapidated old structures. In other words, not a single new public school has been added to the system for a generation, with the result that it now serves only one fourth of the children of school age. A greater number go to private schools, but approximately one third—an estimated quarter of a million children —go to no school at all. Nowhere else in India is the number of the unschooled swelling faster than the total of those who do get enrolled.

The condition of the schools guarantees that there will be no dwindling in the foreseeable future in the masses of the unskilled needing work. As the only major city in eastern India, Calcutta would remain in any case a catch-all for the countryside's surplus labor. With the glut of the unskilled, Calcutta's industrialists long ago became accustomed to paying the lowest industrial wages in India and reaping the highest profits. But in times of scarcity the price of rice in the city is the highest in the country.

Last year it went higher than at any time since the Bengal famine of 1943. Labor unrest and what the industrialists call "indiscipline" then reached floodtide. No doubt, Communist agitators could claim some credit. But what made the agitators effective was the sheer desperation of the workers. Communist trade union leaders soon found they could ride the emotional wave, but couldn't be sure of their ability to control or channel it when it served their purpose to do so. . . .

For months factories and offices were paralyzed by go-slow movements and wildcat strikes. Anyone traveling about the city on errands was almost certain to be delayed by processions of workers angrily chanting revolutionary slogans and waving red banners. Industrialists went to work not knowing whether their workers would allow them to return to their homes at the end of the day. Soon they stopped wearing ties and jackets. "The workers cannot stand to see you wearing good clothes or driving a good car," a shaken employer explained at the time. "They hate it!"

Of the 10 million so-called "man days" lost in the whole of India last year as a result of labor disputes, 6 million were lost in Calcutta alone—one of the few indices on which India's most important business center registered any gain over the rest of the country. . . .

Appropriately, Calcutta's patron deity is Kali—the Hindu goddess of death who represents, according to one commentary, "the supreme night, which swallows all that exists." Kali is normally portrayed as a naked black figure laughing hideously as she dances on a corpse, a raised sword in one of her four hands and a severed head in another. Near her temple here is Kali Ghat, the riverside landing where Calcutta's funeral pyres burn and sputter to ash. Near there also is a new municipal crematorium, which methodically completes the process of disposal that begins on the city's streets.

Most of the crematorium's business comes from one institution in Calcutta that can be said to have confronted the city without blinking—the Home for Dying Destitutes run by Mother Teresa, an Albanian-born nun who dedicates her mission to "the poorest of the poor." The dying are picked up off the streets and taken to the home only after the hospitals refuse to accept them. Many are dazed and unable to give their names.

Their diseases vary; tuberculosis and dysentery are the most common. Hunger is a constant. Mother Teresa and the young Indians in her order bathe, feed and nurse them as best they can. Most important, they give them respect and a chance to end their days with a touch of dignity restored to them. . . .

Saintliness may be the only really adequate response to Calcutta today, but it can never be commonplace. There are many in the city who manage, at least, to become theologians of a kind, devoting endless hours to abstruse debates over how the salvation of revolution can be achieved here. It is reasonable enough for a young man growing up here to conclude that the present Indian system—the uneven, often unseemly blend of parliamentary democracy and old-fashioned colonial administration—has been a failure.

That conclusion turns itself into bitter disdain for those who are running it. And that disdain calls itself revolutionary. But it is one thing to talk about a revolution and another thing to make one. When it comes to revolutionary talk, Calcutta probably ranks second only to Peking. When it comes to actual revolutionary happenings, Calcutta isn't worth mentioning.

# III. TOO MANY PEOPLE, TOO LITTLE FOOD

## EDITOR'S INTRODUCTION

Two dominant problems in the underdeveloped world are the related concerns of too many people and too little food. In recent years, there has been a veritable torrent of articles and books on these questions. Some of what has been written predicts imminent disaster in large parts of the low-income world. Either population will increase so rapidly that some countries will run out of living space or food supplies will fall so far behind needs that mass famine will result. While they in no way minimize the gravity of overpopulation and underproduction, many of the most astute observers nevertheless believe that disaster is neither imminent nor inevitable. The articles in this section attempt to explain the basis for this point of view.

The first essay is by the president of the Population Council. He explains why he has reasonable hope that a solution to the population issue is possible. Perhaps the most basic step—frank acknowledgment of the problem—has already been taken. A decade ago, few countries had formal family-planning programs. Today, many of the underdeveloped countries have such programs. The second article, by the Minister of Health and Family Planning in India, tells what that country is doing or would like to do about limiting its rate of population growth. The third article speaks of the economic gains which would be enjoyed if rates of population increase could be substantially lowered.

The final two articles is this section deal with the complementary question of food production. The first selection tells of the agricultural revolution which has swept parts of Asia in the last few years. The second explores the anatomy of a successful long-term development project in the agricultural field. It also conveys a sense of the difficulties associated with making even a single development project flourish.

## THE POPULATION CRISIS: REASONS FOR HOPE [1]

A discussion of the crisis of population growth must be organized around two sharply contrasting themes: one, of almost unrivaled dangers; the other, of new hope that it may be resolved during the remainder of this century. It is difficult to overstate the importance of either theme. The dangers threaten the entire process of modernization among the two thirds of the world's people in the technologically backward nations, and thereby the maintenance of their political coherence; they threaten, indeed, a catastrophic loss of life. The hope lies in the fact that there is now new reason to think that, if the world is willing to bend its energies toward solving the problems, it can go far toward doing so during the coming decades. The time has passed when the problem must be viewed as insuperable.

In what follows, I shall be concerned with the technologically backward nations. The question here is not what population they might ultimately be capable of supporting if they achieve a high state of development. At present they are desperately poor, grossly uneducated and badly organized to make use of what knowledge they have. They have to start from where they are, and not from where they should like to be. The problem in the real world is that the rate of population growth is proving to be a major obstacle to economic development. Mounting rates of population growth are proving to be almost insuperable obstacles to the technological development on which our future hopes must depend. The heart of the demographic problem is that of slowing the rate of population growth sufficiently to permit the development

[1] From article by Frank W. Notestein, president of the Population Council. *Foreign Affairs.* 46:167-80. O. '67. Reprinted by special permission from *Foreign Affairs,* October 1967. Copyright by the Council on Foreign Relations, Inc., New York.

of the lagging economies and of doing this in the next two
or three decades.

The case is now too well known to require detailed docu-
mentation. Most of the newly developing nations have populations that are growing by at least 2.5 per cent per year.
Moreover, those with slower rates of growth have negligible
health protection and will quickly come to that rate when-
ever rudimentary health services are developed. The rates of
growth go up to 3.5 per cent and occasionally higher. Growth
continuing at 2.5 per cent doubles the size of the population
in twenty-eight years and growth at 3.5 per cent doubles it
in twenty years. In short, unless growth slows down, most of
the technologically backward countries face the problem of
dealing with double their present population well before the
end of the century: that is, well before the children born
this year have completed their own childbearing.

The sources of this rapid growth are easily identified.
Birth rates are very much higher and death rates are very
much lower than they were, for example, in the nineteenth
century period of modernization in Europe. There, populations seldom grew by as much as 1 per cent per year. Whereas in Europe there tended to be about 35 births a year per
1,000 population, in today's newly developing countries birth
rates generally range from 40 to 55. The source of this difference lies mainly in the universality of marriage in the developing nations and in the young ages at which it occurs.

Death rates differ even more spectacularly. In nineteenth
century Europe, death rates of 25 per 1,000 population were
common and a rate as high as 30 was not unusual. In today's
newly developing countries a rate of 25 is very high, 20 is
common and the rates go as low as 6 per 1,000 population.
A primary cause of these low figures is, of course, the new
efficiency with which disease is controlled by sulpha drugs,
antibiotics and insecticides. The expectation of life at birth
has risen remarkably in most of the newly developing countries. Indeed, in a few areas it now exceeds 60 years—not so
very much less than the U.S. figure of 70 years.

The low death rates also come from another and less commonly recognized source. The death rate is simply the annual number of deaths per 1,000 population and therefore is affected by the age composition of the population. Under anything like reasonable health conditions a young population tends to have a low death rate and an old population a high death rate. One of the important reasons that the newly developing countries have low death rates is that their very high birth rates have generated very young populations. It is this that accounts for the fact that the lowest death rates in the world today are found in newly developing countries that have relatively good health services. Taiwan, for example, has a lower death rate than the United States, and Ceylon has a lower death rate than France or England. Moreover, although death rates in the newly developing world are low by historical standards, many remain very high in the light of modern abilities to control disease. Hence we can expect that death rates will continue to be reduced.

It would be unwise, then, to expect even a very rapid decline of birth rates to reduce population growth below 1 per cent by the end of the century. This figure is about the rate of natural increase in the United States at the present time. Barring catastrophe, and under the best possible circumstances, the newly developing world will have to achieve its modernization in spite of rates of population growth running from the present figure of 2.5 to 3.5 per cent down to 1.0 to 1.5 per cent by the end of the century. Any such trend will clearly require a very rapid reduction of birth rates.

The cost of this growth must be met before new investment can be made in educational and productive facilities. The dilemma is now widely understood: if a nation is increasing its product by 5 per cent a year—a level that rather few of the developing nations have thus far been able to sustain—and if its population is growing at 3 per cent per year, then per capita income rises at a rate of 2 per cent. This means that incomes will not have doubled until after the turn of the century. Per capita incomes would rise from, say,

$100 per year to only $200 per year over the next thirty-five years. But, meanwhile, the population would have increased by a factor of 2.7. In short, an excellent economic performance would result in 2.7 times as many people continuing to live in almost abject poverty, with resources for the improvement of education and productive equipment having increased only minimally.

In the densely settled regions of the world the problem is much more difficult than these simple numbers suggest. Consider the situation of India. A perpetuation of its present rate of growth of 2.4 per cent would mean that its present population of about half a billion would rise to one billion before the end of the century. India already faces acute shortages of food. Its agriculture is poorly developed. If it is to support such growth, it must make strenuous efforts to enhance the production of the land. A rapid but theoretically possible development of agricultural technology should enable India to meet at least its minimum needs. But to increase production in this fashion requires very little more labor. It requires instead the rationalization of agriculture through development of better crop practices, transportation, credit facilities, pest control and fertilization. It does not require more people. And yet if its present population growth continues, India faces the problem of finding—within about twenty-nine years—the means to support another half billion people outside of agriculture. In an era of rising expectations how long can political coherence be maintained in the presence of unemployment on a possibly unprecedented scale?

If political coherence cannot be maintained, the risks change—from those of growth to those of a catastrophic loss of life. The margins of safety are pathetically thin. It would not take much disorganization to block transportation and public health activities so that famine and epidemic disease would stalk the land. To anyone inclined to point out that this would at least be one solution to the problems of population pressure, the reply must be that massive upheavals also jeopardize every aspect of the development process and every hope of representative government in unregimented societies. The risks of events of this kind are real in such densely settled areas as India, Pakistan, Indonesia and Egypt. Mainland China, about which we know very little, may already be experiencing these catastrophes.

In view of the foregoing it may seem reckless to turn to the optimistic side of the picture, but there is such a side which I think is persuasive....

In this hopeful judgment four elements are important: (1) the development of national policies favoring family planning; (2) the demonstrated public interest in limiting childbearing; (3) the improvement of contraceptive technology; and (4) the fact that for the first time in history several Oriental populations have begun to cut their birth rates as a result of governmental programs to spread the practice of birth control....

A decade ago, India was the only country that had adopted a national policy to promote the practice of family planning, although for several years the plan had more words than substance. Today, more than half the people of the newly developing world live under governments that have decided to reduce their birth rates by family planning. These include Mainland China, Nepal, Pakistan, India, Ceylon, Malaysia, Indonesia (if still a bit ambiguously), Singapore, Hong Kong, Taiwan (in deed, if not in word), South Korea, Iran, Turkey, Egypt, Tunisia, Morocco, Kenya, Barbados, Jamaica and Honduras. Many other countries, such as Colombia and Chile, are setting up active governmental and quasi-governmental programs. In still other countries substantial efforts are going on in universities, public hospitals and in local health departments. These include, for example, Thailand, the Philippines and Venezuela.

It must immediately be said that a governmental policy does not guarantee an effective program; there has often been a lag of several years between the adoption of a policy and the beginning of effective work. The point, however, is one of future relevance. The fact is that the newly developing nations have themselves been coming to an awareness of the seriousness of their population problems and of the extent to which their best work in economic development is being frustrated by too rapid increases in the numbers of their people. Their awakening to the urgency of the problem has come with remarkable and accelerating speed. . . .

The second reason for optimism concerning the possibilities of reducing rates of population growth is that the public has been shown to be interested in limiting family size. The finding is surprising, for students of traditional agrarian societies have long reported that motivation for restricting fertility generally is not high. Many of the attitudes, customs, beliefs and familial arrangements remain those of centuries past in which survival, not overrapid growth, posed the problem. These factors continue today to weaken interest in family planning.

Nevertheless, sample surveys conducted in some twenty developing countries show that, without exception, substantial majorities of married couples want to restrict their childbearing. Moreover, these attitudes are found in the villages as well as in the cities—among illiterates as well as among the educated. The women want to limit their childbearing, not necessarily to only two or three children, for they may often want four or five and at least one son. But they want to curtail their childbearing, and this attitude is widespread even in communities in which there is little evidence of modernization.

Actually, these communities often have a great deal more modernization than first strikes the eye of the prosperous Western visitor. His overwhelming impression is that of poverty. But the villager has movies (either regularly or through traveling theaters), transistor radios and a desire to educate his children. He is aware that his children no longer die in infancy as they used to do, that sweeping epidemics no longer appear. He is also aware that more surviving children mean more difficulty in providing enough food, and he sees that today a medium-sized family will provide enough surviving adults to protect him in his old age. All these factors have increased the proportion of couples who say that they would like to practice contraception.

The demonstration of interest is based on much more than responses to surveys. In many societies a large number of crude and illegal abortions gives eloquent testimony to the motivations for restriction. Moreover, wherever there have been well-organized contraceptive services through which information and supplies are readily available, the response has been large. Where there is indifference, it usually has been to poorly organized services poorly supported by educational effort. Any lack of interest on the part of the public is less serious than the apathy of the middle classes and the lesser officials who cannot bring themselves to believe that their illiterate peasants are sufficiently intelligent to understand their own problems. Both surveys and the public response to services clearly demonstrate that ordinary people have a much better understanding of their own problems than their lesser officials appreciate.

The third encouraging fact is the improvement of contraceptive technology. During the past decade we have gained two methods which are safe, cheap and highly effective, and that for the first time make no demands on the couple at the time of coition. One is the new plastic intrauterine device (IUD) that, once inserted, remains indefinitely in place for those who tolerate it. Experience with it varies, depending on the quality of service and the extent to which the patient is warned to expect some initial discomfort. The weight of evidence is that with reasonable care (including reinsertion in some patients who expel it) some 55 or 60 per cent of women continue to be completely protected after two years. The other 40 to 45 per cent include women whose husbands have died, those who have decided to have a child and those who prefer other methods; only 20 to 30 per cent cannot tolerate or retain it. The rate of pregnancy among users, including women who have unknowingly expelled the device, is 2 to 3 a year per hundred women. This is less than half the rate with conventional contraceptives under the best conditions.

The oral steroids [birth control pills] offer the other most promising method. Until recently, they were too expensive to meet the needs of the majority in the developing countries. Recently, however, prices for bulk orders have dropped to about 15 cents per cycle, which permits their use in governmental programs, at least for those patients who cannot use the IUD. When the pill is systematically taken it is absolutely effective. We do not yet know how effective it is in actual use or what proportion of women will continue to use it. Preliminary indications in Taiwan and Korea are that the rates of discontinuation are, if anything, somewhat higher than those with the IUD. . . .

The fourth reason for optimism about the possibility of reducing birth rates is that some countries have already done so. This is the case in South Korea, Taiwan, Hong Kong and Singapore, and perhaps in other countries where the evidence is more difficult to marshal.

South Korea offers no accurate birth rates, but consider the indirect evidence that they are falling. Last year over 390,000 women had IUD's inserted, bringing the total in the two-and-a-half-year program through 1966 to 737,000. Since 1962 there have been at least 80,000 male sterilizations. At the end of 1966 about 170,000 couples were receiving conventional contraceptive supplies from government stations. Altogether, with allowance for duplications, something like 900,000 couples have been served by the government effort. Since the program began (mostly since 1963), more than 20 per cent of the women of childbearing age have taken part, and surveys indicate that about 20 per cent of all couples are currently practicing contraception. Moreover, growing acceptance continues in 1967 with no indication that a saturation point has been reached.

According to year-end population registrations, of admittedly defective quality, the ratio of children under age five to women of childbearing age shows a sharp decline between 1962 and 1965, both nationally and in every province of the country. The Planning Board believes that the rate of natural increase has dropped from an estimated 3 per cent in 1962 to about 2.5 per cent in 1966; it has set a target of 2 per cent by 1971. Clearly the birth rate has begun to fall rapidly in response to a strong governmental program.

In Taiwan the birth rate has been dropping for the last ten years, from 45 per 1,000 in 1955 to 34.5 in 1964, 32.7 in 1965 and to a record low of 32.4 in 1966. (The actual and comparable figure would have been below 31 if a census in December 1966 had not brought in early birth registrations and omissions from the previous years.) The goal is to reach a birth rate of 20 by 1973. The program has depended heavily on the IUD. . . . The fertility rates of women twenty-five to twenty-nine are beginning to drop and the proportion of IUD acceptors with only three children is rising. The fact that 37 per cent of the IUD patients have discontinued after eighteen months has led to efforts to improve the service and to make pills available. It appears, however, that even those who discontinue the IUD control their fertility rather effectively. . . .

The glow of optimism that can come from considering these successful programs fades when we consider India and Pakistan. Those nations have had appropriate policies, but they cannot yet point to reduced birth rates with any certainty. It has been only in the last two or three years that the programs have had much substance. Now they are getting under way, and by the end of this year India will apparently have inserted more than two million IUD's and Pakistan nearly one million. In both countries sterilization is beginning to take a significant place, and work with pills is beginning. If the programs continue to go forward at the new pace the efforts can become highly significant in a few years. . . .

Newly developed nations offer examples of rapidly falling birth rates. Japan's birth rate, for example, had dropped by last year from a postwar high of 34 per 1,000 to 14;

Japan now shares with Hungary the lowest birth rate in the world. The decline was not the result of a governmental birth-control program; it was mainly due to abortion rather than contraception, and came almost in spite of the government. The public took such enthusiastic advantage of abortion permitted by the "Eugenic Protection Law" that it was politically impossible to interpret the law narrowly. At present there is a marked trend away from abortion and toward contraception, but Japan has shown that population growth can be drastically reduced by a prosperous people having few inhibitions against abortion and served by a competent medical establishment. The Japanese medical community's enthusiasm for abortion has seeped into Taiwan, South Korea, Hong Kong and Singapore, though it remains illegal.

Abortion is legal in the U.S.S.R. and all of Eastern Europe except East Germany and Albania. As in Japan, it has been a major factor in reducing birth rates which were high before the war but now are for the most part lower than in the United States. Abortion is apparently legal under many circumstances in Mainland China, and there is a good deal of talk about making it legal in India and Pakistan. In view of the dearth of medical personnel and facilities and the improved efficiency of modern contraceptives, it is doubtful that abortion will play the major role in reducing population growth in India and the Moslem world that it did in Japan, the Soviet Union and Eastern Europe.

Abortion is, nevertheless, important today. In Turkey, where until two years ago contraception was illegal, the Ministry of Health estimates that more than one in four pregnancies is terminated by illegal abortion. In Latin America, where church opposition has held back the development of governmental contraceptive services, abortion is rife. . . .

This, then, is the optimistic case for saying that the newly developing countries can, if they will, bring their rates of population growth to reasonably low levels in the next two or three decades provided that they have the needed assistance from international, governmental and private agencies in the developed world. In absolute terms the assistance needed from the developed world is large, but it is small compared to that needed for economic development. Aid should include help with training at the professional and subprofessional levels in a wide range of biological, medical and social science specialties; assistance in building and enriching the medical infrastructure on which contraceptive services depend; assistance with organization, logistics, supplies and materials for informational and educational programs. Basic and applied research that seeks to attain new efficiency in the regulation of fertility needs to be increased throughout the world. . . .

Whatever happens, it is probable that, short of a major rise in the death rate, population growth will not be stopped for some decades. Given the necessary effort, however, it does seem likely that growth will be reduced to levels that can be coped with in a world of rapidly developing science and technology. In the long run, of course, growth must stop. Quite possibly it will not do so even if every couple is able to limit its childbearing to the precise number of children it wants. But a world in which all couples are able to choose the size of their family will be a world in which an alteration of institutional constraints would prove rather quickly effective. If the developing nations can move from their present growth rates of 2.5 and 3.5 per cent to 1 and 1.5 per cent while health improves, the problems will not all be solved, but the crisis will be passed.

It would be a great mistake to suppose that we will move into the future with a linear extension of past performance. No one ten years ago would have forecast the rapid changes of the past decade in policies, in contraceptive technology, in public interest and in programmatic successes. We must assume that the future will bring an accelerated pace of change. We have already moved from a position of public apathy to one of deep concern by many people. Today, governments, international agencies and private organizations are talking a great deal about major efforts and new groups are entering the discourse every day. Everything on the horizon suggests a further deepening of interest, both public and private. Our estimate of the future possibilities should be based on the premise that we are at the beginning of an accelerating trend. Almost all of the actual work, national and international, remains to be done. If our efforts are commensurate with our opportunities, however, we have reason to believe that by the end of the century the specter of poverty perpetuated by population growth can be lifted from the earth.

## HOW INDIA IS TACKLING
## HER POPULATION PROBLEM [2]

The government of India and its . . . citizens have been aware of the problems posed by the rapid growth of India's population during the past decade and a half; but the adverse economic circumstances [poor harvests] of the last two or three years brought home to them, as nothing had done in the past, the disturbing nature of India's population explosion. The psychological climate necessary for the serious implementation of the family-planning program had arrived.

The dimensions and magnitude of India's population problem may be briefly recalled. India's total population passed the 520 million mark in mid-1968. That is, one out of every seven persons in the world is a citizen of India. With only 2.4 per cent of the world's total land area, India has to support 14 per cent of the world's total population. To this population a baby is born every second and a half, 21 million births a year, a birth rate of 41 per thousand per year. Some 8 million persons die every year—a high death rate of 16 per thousand per year. Thus the nation adds 13 million people—Australia's present population—to the existing population every year. The population is growing at the rate of slightly

[2] From article by S. Chandrasekhar, Minister of Health and Family Planning in India. *Foreign Affairs.* 47:138-50. O. '68. Reprinted by special permission from *Foreign Affairs,* October 1968. Copyright by the Council on Foreign Relations, Inc., New York.

over 2.5 per cent per year. And at the current rate of increase it may double itself in the next twenty-eight years, reaching the incredible figure of one billion before the end of this century.

The major cause of this high rate of growth is not so much the high birth rate as the increasing success, in terms of Asian standards, with which India's health and medical services have been implemented in the last three five-year plans. Major communicable diseases like cholera, malaria and smallpox have been nearly brought under control and measures to eradicate them are now being put into effect. And, in response to these relatively improved health conditions, life expectancy has risen from 32 years in 1950 to 51 years in 1968.

But India has also registered remarkable progress in both the agricultural and industrial sectors during the last twenty years of her political freedom. This progress, far exceeding anything registered during any comparable earlier period, is all the more significant considering the heavy odds and unprecedented problems that the new government of India had to face, ranging all the way from the forced Hindu migration from Pakistan into India, which involved the settlement and rehabilitation of millions of refugees, to the brief but costly border wars with Communist China and Pakistan. In addition, the food problem has been a cause of considerable anxiety, especially over the past few years.

Although the availability of goods and services has increased threefold over the last decade, their per capita consumption has not increased at all. While this year a partial breakthrough in agricultural production has been achieved, resulting in bumper crops of nearly 100 million tons, compared to about 65 million tons a year in the past few years, the per capita consumption of food grains has not markedly increased. As for educational facilities, the number of universities has increased from 16 in 1947 to 67 in 1968, and the liberal arts colleges affiliated to these universities have increased proportionately—an impressive achievement. But thousands of students with the requisite academic credentials continue to find it difficult to secure admission to these colleges. The increased facilities simply do not keep pace with the needs of the growing population. This is true of almost every aspect of life in India. . . .

The main reason why the Indian economy continues to be an economy of shortages is the country's excessive population growth. Between mid-1947 when India gained her political freedom and mid-1968 she has added 182.7 million to her total population. Like other underdeveloped countries, India bears witness to the fact that the technology of health and hygiene can be more rapidly transmitted than the technology of production and economic growth. This means that the population increases rapidly as a result of death control, but the increase in the production of food and other necessities does not keep pace.

## II

Hence the declared objective of the government of India to reduce the birth rate from the present 41 per thousand to 25—if not 20—per thousand as expeditiously as possible. Although a policy of population control has been in force for the last few years, it was only after the formation of the new cabinet early in 1967 that a vigorous, new antinatalist policy was formulated and an all-out campaign begun to halve the nation's birth rate by 1975-76 if possible.

This population policy has to be made effective within the framework of an open society with centuries-old customs and traditions. India today is the largest democracy in the world, but an overwhelming majority of the people are illiterate (more than 70 per cent), are small-scale farmers (about 80 per cent), and live in some 564,000 far-flung villages; some 14 major languages and more than 200 dialects are in use. The cultural levels of the population vary all the way from a Nobel-prize winner to a preliterate peasant. What is more, according to the constitution, health and family planning are responsibilities of the states. Since the efficiency

of the administrative machinery of the various state governments is not uniform, there are considerable differences in
the achievement of family-planning targets.

The major problem before the government is to reach the
country's married couples and convince them of the need
for small families. During the last twenty years we have conducted some thirty surveys of attitudes of parents among
rural and urban populations, comprising various caste, religious, cultural and income groups. A summary of these
random samplings shows that about 70 per cent of wives and
about 66 per cent of husbands among couples with at least
three children are in favor of family planning for economic
and health reasons. It may be assumed, then, that a majority
of Indian couples is in favor, at least in principle, of family
planning. Of the 105 million married couples in the country
today, living together and leading a normal conjugal life,
90 million couples are in the reproductive age group; and
these are our target couples who must be brought to accept
the small-family norm. They are distributed over 17 states,
11 union territories (comparable to the District of Columbia),
326 administrative districts, some 2,690 towns and cities and
564,258 villages. In each of India's 17 states (except four
Hindi-speaking states) a different language is spoken and
each can be considered a country in itself. Indeed, if the state
of Uttar Pradesh were to join the United Nations, its population of a little over 80 million would make it the seventh
largest member.

India's towns and cities are well knit and it is not difficult
to reach their inhabitants. They have government hospitals
and clinics, schools and colleges; they are served by railroads
and many are connected by airways. Literacy rates are high,
newspapers and periodicals are read avidly, and people listen
to All-India Radio. But our communications program nevertheless has to take into account wide differences in culture,
religion, custom and tradition. To carry it through we have
set up a media section in the Health and Family Planning
Ministry. The basic approach is to present only a few simple

messages, in a few words, repeated in the same form in all possible media. An example of this approach is the use of the happy faces of the "family of four" with the slogan "Two or three children—enough" and the Red Triangle to identify the program and the location of family-planning facilities. This simple message is being propagated through motion pictures, on the radio, through a family-planning song, in the press, on billboards, posters, cinema slides and on the sides of buses.

But the villages pose a problem; and it is the 60 million farm couples, illiterate and poor, who need family planning most. Talks, group discussions and *Bhajans* (religious musical discourses) on family planning have been promoted; and peripatetic clinics have been organized in rural areas. But although radio should be the most effective instrument of our propaganda, the community radio sets . . . are frequently out of order. . . .

### III

Perhaps the most difficult problem before us is the choice of a contraceptive that is acceptable under Indian conditions, particularly in the depressed rural areas where privacy, running water, electricity, and knowledge of reproductive physiology and, most important, motivation, are more or less absent. Besides, among such diverse groups no single method, however good, can be suitable to all. Hence, we have adopted what we call the cafeteria approach: theoretically all the scientifically approved contraceptives are available to the people in the Government Family Planning clinics, but for mass consumption only four methods are now advocated and made available.

The first of these is sterilization—vasectomy for fathers or tubectomy for mothers. Vasectomy, the simple operation on the male, which I popularized in Madras State fifteen years ago, has now caught on and is becoming popular. Generally Indian couples marry early and have three or four children; they then want a simple and permanent method of conception control. Sometimes, when the husband is unwilling, the wife may undergo tubectomy, which is a relatively major operation needing at least a week's hospitalization. All services are free—the surgeon's fee, the hospital and drugs, and in addition a few rupees are given to the patient to offset the loss of wages and incidental expenses. These few rupees—about five dollars—have assumed the nature of an incentive. In fact, in large industrial establishments . . . , workers who are willing to undergo vasectomy after the third child are offered an incentive of 250 rupees—and a few days' leave with pay. Up to mid-June 1968, 4.2 million persons had been sterilized. Ninety per cent of these sterilizations are vasectomies and the rest are tubectomies.

The second widespread method is the IUD (intrauterine contraceptive device), or the loop, introduced in 1965. So far 2.4 million loops have been inserted. But the method is not very popular as it has led to excessive bleeding in about 10 per cent of the cases, as well as involuntary expulsion in about 6 per cent. Research to devise a better loop is under way. All the needed loops are manufactured in India in a government-owned factory.

The third contraceptive method we are advocating is the condom or sheath. The total requirement is well above 300 million pieces per annum, and so far indigenous production totals only about 30 million. The rest have to be imported, involving foreign exchange. However, in 1968 we have been able to obtain from the United States Government, as a part of its aid to India's Family Planning Program, 200 million sheaths. In addition, we have set up a factory owned by the government of India—the Hindustan Latex Limited—in Kerala, with technical assistance from Japan and the United States. This concern will go into production in a few months and will produce 145 million pieces a year.

But apart from production there is also a marketing problem. We have to devise a distribution mechanism to reach the people in our far-flung rural communities, where demand has to be created and supplies provided. Of course, all hospitals, clinics and Family Welfare Centers carry all supplies and distribute them free. Another distribution channel is through postmen, school teachers and members of cooperative societies; they receive the condoms free and in turn sell them at a nominal rate of 5 paise (less than a cent) for three pieces, keeping the proceeds as commission. Thus a large number of people who otherwise would not go to the Family Planning Centers are reached. . . .

The latest contraceptive method we are making available is the pill. My predecessor was opposed to including the pill in the official family-planning program, but after discussions with experts in the World Health Organization and the USAID [United States Agency for International Development] I have approved its use. Since we do not manufacture the pill in India, the import cost in hard currency was a matter of some concern. But during my discussions with President Johnson and USAID officials earlier this year in Washington, generous American dollar aid to our program was forthcoming and has made it posible for us to embark on a pilot project in which about 100,000 highly motivated urban wives are put on the pill under medical supervision. If the pill proves successful, its use may be extended.

Family-planning methods and the necessary supplies and advice are available in 26,202 centers all over the country, made up of 1,815 urban centers, 5,133 main rural centers and 19,254 rural subcenters. In addition, 1,592 hospitals and urban institutions and 7,401 rural institutions do family-planning work. The federal government has taken the necessary steps to provide male and female doctors for these centers. So far, 13,087 doctors have been trained in various family-planning methods to work in the centers and some 120,520 paramedical personnel have been trained to assist the doctors.

But the paucity of doctors, particularly women doctors trained in family planning and willing to work in rural areas, continues to be an acute problem. In fact, we are faced with the perennial problem of finding trained workers at all levels

—whether nurses, health educators or health visitors. But by dint of scholarships to medical students who opt to work in family planning and special emoluments for doctors working in rural hardship posts we hope to meet this difficulty.

## IV

What factors—political, economic, social and religious—favor our current efforts to reduce India's birth rate? The foremost factor is the government's awareness that population growth is the nation's number-one problem, ranking with the question of modernizing India's agriculture and food production. Indeed, food production and family planning are simply two sides of the coin of national economic and social development. Awareness of this fact has led to the creation of the largest official family-planning program of its kind in the world. . . .

During the first Five-Year Plan (1951-1956) a small sum of 3 million rupees was appropriated for family planning, but the health ministry's energies in popularizing the rhythm method were so misspent that only . . . [half that amount] was actually used over the five years and only 147 family-planning clinics were set up. During the second Five-Year Plan (1956-1961) 22 million rupees were spent and the number of clinics increased to 4,165. The third Five-Year Plan (1961-1966) witnessed the introduction of all methods of family planning, including the loop, disseminated through the extension education approach. For the fourth Five-Year Plan begun in 1966 and currently being discussed, a tentative sum of 23,000 million rupees is proposed. Under today's program, there are one Primary Health Center for 80,000 of rural population and one urban center for 50,000 population. . . .

During the last year and a half, international assistance, support and sympathy for our program have increased. Aid, large and small, is coming from the United States ($30 million), Sweden ($2.2 million), Japan and Denmark. Several foreign agencies have also helped, the largest aid coming from the Ford Foundation. This foreign assistance covers a wide variety of programs—provision of technical experts, commodities and supplies and training for our personnel both in India and abroad. A random listing includes vehicles, audiovisual equipment, paper, printing and mailing units, films, condoms, oral contraceptives, raw materials, training and research facilities.

## V

However, there are some unfavorable factors with which we have to contend. Perhaps the most distressing of these is the injection of communal and religious bias into the program. While we have made every effort to keep it truly national, above and beyond party and religious politics, certain opposition parties attack us on the ground that its actual implementation is changing the ratio among the existing religious groups. The argument frequently voiced by the Jana Sangh, the right extremist Hindu opposition party, contends that considerably more Hindus than Muslims (in relation to their respective total populations) are being sterilized. And, secondly, since Hindus are bound by the monogamic law while Muslims are permitted to have four wives according to their law, the total population of the Hindus is likely to dwindle while that of the Muslims is likely to increase rapidly. Since in a democracy numbers matter and since many vote on the basis of religious (and caste) loyalties, the present family-planning program might eventually change the entire complexion of the Indian (Hindu) nation. So runs the argument.

Our reply is that Muslims, Christians (both Protestant and Catholic) and other minority religious communities are all coming to the government clinics and that the command ratio of the Indian population shows no signs of changing. All evidence shows that these Hindu extremist fears are groundless and that educated and motivated husbands and wives resort to family planning while the very poor, the ignorant and the unmotivated do not—among all religious groups. . . .

Another serious difficulty is the want of an efficient, modernized and national welfare-oriented administrative machinery. The present bureaucracy owes its existence to the British rulers, who were understandably interested in maintaining law and order and collecting revenues. . . .

There is also some cultural resistance to family planning among certain communities, particularly in rural areas. The desire of Hindu parents for sons is well known. A couple with two sons, for instance, is highly motivated in favor of family planning, but a couple with five daughters would like to try again for a son. This desire for sons is in part a religious attitude, but basically it corresponds to an economic need, for with farming completely unmechanized a villager needs sons as workers on his farm. The village couple with two or three children but only one son is often reluctant to practice family planning on the grounds that, given the high rate of child mortality, their son might not survive the critical first five years. This very real problem argues the need for the intensive program now being launched in India to combat malnutrition (the basis of most child mortality) among preschool-age children. In this group malnutrition is a qualitative as well as a quantitative problem and calls for a reduction in nutrient deficiencies through food fortification (wheat, rice and salt), low-cost formulated foods, and large-scale child-feeding programs. A recent study estimates that nearly 70 per cent of the childhood malnutrition in India could be eliminated by the limitation of families to three children. . . .

## VI

Such are the major features of India's current program to cut down its birth rate. Two further proposals which will help reduce the country's total fertility have been before us for some time and will now go before Parliament in the form of bills to raise the age of consent for girls and to liberalize abortion.

It is an established fact that either as a result of being generally more mature, or because of greater opportunities for education and for gainful employment, or a combination of these, girls marrying at a later age favor and adopt family planning more readily. There is a correlation between raising the marriage age of our girls and reducing the nation's birth rate. Marrying at a higher age cuts down the reproductive span. Some recent studies have shown that if the minimum age at marriage for females were fixed at 20 years the reduction in the birth rate in a decade would range from 12 to 30 per cent.

The minimum age at marriage for girls, fixed at fourteen by the Child Marriage Restraint Act of 1929, was raised to fifteen in 1957. We are hoping to raise it to eighteen years. Opposition is not lacking, for some critics maintain that this may cause hardship to rural girls who have no educational opportunities and who marry—the only career open to them —as early as they can. But we feel that Parliament will approve the proposed measure in view of the pressing need to reduce the nation's birth rate.

The second proposal before us is to liberalize the existing law on abortion. The provisions regarding abortion in the Indian Penal Code were enacted about a century ago, in keeping with the British Law on the subject. Abortion was made a crime for which the mother as well as the abortionist could be punished in all cases except where it had to be induced in order to save the mother's life. This law has been observed in the breach in a very large number of cases in rural and urban areas all over India. Whatever may be the moral and ethical feelings professed by some sections of society on the question of induced abortion, it is an undeniable fact that large numbers of Indian mothers are prepared to risk their lives in an illegal abortion rather than carry that particular child to term. Furthermore, it is revealed that a great majority of these mothers are married women.

The main argument in India against liberalizing abortion is that the strain on the existing medical services would be too great. But a recent breakthrough in the Soviet Union would soon make this argument out of date. Soviet scientists have prepared an aborting device . . . which is virtually harmless and does not need special surgical supervision.

## GAINS FROM POPULATION CONTROL [3]

In the contemporary situation, four aspects of the population problem in the less-developed areas are operating to retard economic development. These are the relatively high rate of population growth, unfavorable age structure, imbalanced population distribution and inadequately educated and trained manpower. All of these obstructions to economic development are amenable to control. But they cannot be controlled unless the ways in which they hamper efforts to raise standards of living are fully understood, relevant policies are formulated and necessary programs put into operation. . . .

The standard of living cannot be raised unless total output increases more rapidly than total population. The greater the rate of population increase, the higher must be the rate of economic growth to effect any increase in per capita income.

Given their projected rates of population growth, the less-developed regions must achieve unprecedented increases in GNP over the next three and a half decades to equal, by 2000, the standards of living in Northern and Western Europe as they were in 1962. That is, Asia must achieve a sustained annual economic growth rate of about 9 per cent, Africa, about 10 per cent and Latin America, about 7 per cent. Similarly, given their projected population increases, Asia and Africa, to match the higher 1962 North American

[3] From *World Population Problems,* pamphlet by P. M. Hauser, population expert. (Headline Series no 174) Foreign Policy Association. 345 E. 46th St. New York 10017. D. '65. p 23-31. Copyright 1965 by Foreign Policy Association, Inc. Reprinted by permission.

standard of living by the year 2000, must achieve a GNP growth rate of about 11 per cent per annum for the remainder of the century and Latin America, a GNP growth of about 9 per cent per annum.

The magnitude of this task should be evident. In fact, unless the rates of population growth in the underdeveloped areas diminish, they cannot possibly match 1962 European standards of living, let alone the North American level, by the end of the century. At best, given their projected rates of population growth, they can achieve only meager advances in living standards.

With rapid population growth there is a need for capital investment to achieve economic advance. To effect a step-up in output, additional investment must be great enough to produce income increments adequate to raise per capita income. Capital-income ratios indicate that to obtain an added unit of income, approximately three units of capital are required. Populations increasing at a rate of 3 per cent per year, already approximated by Latin America and other parts of the world and in prospect for most of the less-developed areas in this century, must therefore achieve a saving and investment of approximately 9 per cent per annum merely to maintain their present low levels of per capita income. Yet many of the economically less-developed societies find it difficult to achieve a savings rate of more than 4 to 5 per cent. It is doubtful that India, even with its prodigious efforts toward economic development, has as yet achieved a savings rate in excess of 10 per cent. Thus, even with outside capital, it has found the task of keeping ahead of its 2 per cent per annum increase in population most difficult. This is why India has increased its efforts to control population growth.

Rapid population increase, it must be observed, is not necessarily a barrier to economic development. There can be little doubt that at certain stages in the history of the present economically advanced nations it has actually contributed to higher standards of living. But the man-resources ratio in these nations was, on the whole, much more favorable at their initial stages of economic growth than is true of many less-developed areas today. In North America during the nineteenth century, a resource-rich unexploited continent, rapid population increase undoubtedly contributed to increased standards of living. For with its low man-resources ratio, rapid population growth contributed to economies of large-scale production. In those less-developed areas today where there is already a high man-resources ratio, rapid population growth contributes not to economies of large-scale production, but to diminishing returns. However, it should be noted that in those developing areas where population densities are still low, rapid growth may contribute to economic growth provided capital and other inputs can meet the population challenge.

## Unfavorable Age Structure

High fertility areas have larger proportions of young persons than do low fertility areas. In most of the underdeveloped countries about 40 per cent or more of the total population is under fifteen years of age. In contrast, in Europe and in North America between 25 and 30 per cent of the total population is under fifteen years of age. Continued high fertility and rapid population growth in the developing areas will mean continuation of the relatively high proportion of young people.

The relatively large proportion of persons under fifteen years of age in the less-developed regions of the world may be interpreted as "unfavorable" to economic development for at least two reasons. First, it tends to reduce labor input per capita and, all other things being equal, tends therefore to reduce income per capita. Second, it requires that a greater part of limited resources be allocated to "social" investment rather than to "economic" investment. That is, the more youthful the population the greater is the proportion of total savings that must be devoted to the rearing of the

young and the smaller is the proportion available for investment in agricultural or industrial projects.

It should be noted that changes in age structure are the
result of changes in mortality as well as in fertility. Reductions in the death rate occur first of all and disproportion-
ately among infants and youths. In consequence, reduced
mortality tends to increase greatly the proportion of young
persons in a population. Reductions in the birth rate, on the
contrary, tend to decrease the proportion of young persons
in a population. Over a period of time the effect of reduced
birth rates will more than offset that of reduced mortality,
and the proportion of older people will increase.

A UN study has analyzed the effect of reductions in fertility and mortality on the active male workers who must
produce the wealth necessary to support the needs of the
whole population. This study shows that reduction of mortality increases the burden of the workers, whereas the reduction of fertility reduces it. All other things being equal,
the greater the ratio of workers in a population the greater
will be its income per capita.

High fertility, then, under conditions of declining mortality, has the effect of retarding economic development. It
not only is responsible for high rates of total population
growth, but also produces an age structure which adversely
affects economic growth.

*Imbalance in Population Distribution*

Industrialization inevitably leads to increasing urbanization. However, the less-developed areas of Asia, Latin America and Africa, because they have such a vast total population, have more people living in cities of twenty thousand or
more than do the industrialized nations of Europe and
North America combined. In 1950 Asia, Latin America and
Africa contained over 45 per cent of the world's residents
of cities of twenty thousand or more; whereas Europe (excluding the U.S.S.R.) and North America contained but 41
per cent living in cities of this size.

The implications of urbanization for the advanced and for the less-developed nations are different. In the former, urbanization is both an antecedent and a consequence of high standards of living. It makes possible and promotes the division of labor and specialization, with resulting higher per capita income. However, in the newly developing areas, urbanization tends to be the product of quite different factors and is not accompanied by corresponding increases in productivity and living standards. It is less the result of indigenous economic development and the pull to the urban centers because of greater economic opportunity than a reflection of the push from overpopulated rural areas. . . .

Compared with the advanced nations at similar levels of urbanization, a much smaller proportion of the labor force in the developing nations is engaged in nonagricultural and especially mechanized industrial occupations. Such areas face a difficult problem in attaining levels of economic development adequate to support their present, let alone their prospective, urban populations.

Given the present levels of productivity and limited savings in the less-developed areas, a major common problem relates to the allocation of resources for the improvement of agriculture, on the one hand, and the development of industrial sectors of the economy, on the other. In many nations improvement in agricultural productivity may contribute more to rising standards of living than efforts to induce industrialization. The claims of large and politically important urban populations may require disproportionate allocations of limited resources to the development of the urban, rather than the agricultural, sectors of the economy.

The achievement of adequate balance between agricultural and urban industrial development is complicated by difficult problems of dividing limited savings between "social" and "productive" investment. This problem finds its most acute form in the city. Urban areas in the less-developed nations are characterized by inadequate infrastructure development which precludes the usual amenities of city existence found in advanced nations. There is a great need and much temptation to allocate resources to social purposes such as the elimination of shanty towns, piped water, sewage, better housing and social services for newcomers. Investment of this type, badly needed as it may be, can be made only at the expense of decreased investment in agricultural and industrial productive facilities. . . .

### Quality of Human Resources

Population has two dimensions: quantity and quality. Thus far we have been concerned with problems of quantity. Still another problem in the underdeveloped areas is the low general educational level and low skills of the population at large and, most importantly, of the labor force. High levels of illiteracy and the absence of a skilled labor force serve as major barriers to economic growth, particularly in the urban and industrial sectors of the economy.

It is becoming recognized that perhaps the most important single type of investment for achieving economic development is investment in human resources. In fact, many economists argue that investment in education and skills may provide a greater return than any other input. Moreover, evidence is mounting that only a relatively small part of increased output is the result of increases in the conventionally regarded inputs of labor, land and capital combined. For example, recent studies suggest that for the period 1899-1953 in the United States, only a third of increased output may be accounted for by increased input of labor, land and capital. The remaining two thirds seems to be the result of the combination of technology, organization and investment in humans, together with all other factors. Moreover, the data suggest that of these latter types of input, investment in humans, that is, in the improved quality of population through more education and training, may be the most important. . . .

An impoverished nation, with uncontrolled fertility, has a smaller per capita investment available for education. The

ous than Frenchmen. The country is, of course, well known as offering one of the outstanding examples of successful development. In two decades Mexico has more than tripled its output of goods and services and has raised the real per capita income of its people by three fourths. Its industries are growing rapidly. Over the last ten years the average annual increase in gross national product has been of the order of 6 per cent. Mexico's 46 million people, about equally divided between town and country, are increasing in numbers by 3.5 per cent each year—one of the fastest growth rates in the world. Although this rate is alarming to some demographers, it does not seem to disturb the Mexicans, whose pervasive sense of national destiny causes them to speak proudly of the day—not too far distant—when there will be 80 million Mexicans—the better to share in a future which looks full of promise.

### Colonia Michoacán

In the late 1940's, a group of farmers from the state of Michoacán in central Mexico packed such goods as they possessed, left their rocky little parcels of land, and began a long trek to the Northwest where, they had heard, things were better and there was promise of a new life. They came to start an *ejido*—a Mexican institution which has features of both a cooperative and a collective farm. . . .

Colonia Michoacán—as the village is called—a community of about three hundred families, lies on flat land ribbed by irrigation canals, about thirty kilometers from Culiacán, the state capital. Most of the villagers' houses are built of stucco or cement blocks. The streets are straight and well canted for drainage. The best building in town is the school —from kindergarten through the sixth grade—and though most of the children leave after the sixth grade a few go on to the secondary school in Culiacán. Colonia Michoacán is electrified, has its own plant for purifying drinking water and has a machinery pool consisting of trucks, harvesters, tractors, and assorted implements. When the farmers need their crops dusted, they contract with a nearby agricultural flying service. The typical house is sparsely furnished, but many have electric refrigerators, irons, and fans, and almost all have electric light. Stoves fueled by bottled gas have for the most part replaced charcoal and kerosene cookers. And, if human progress can be measured by the ratio of television sets to population, it is perhaps worth noting that there are 17 television sets in the village.

The people—particularly the younger ones—look healthy. A medical clinic, operated by the government, is 12 kilometers away. The villagers say that the care is good, but they complain about the time it takes to get an appointment. They also complain about inflation (they say the cost of living has increased 30 per cent in the last five years), the low price they got for rice this year [1968], the high cost of credit, and about occasional shortages of irrigation water. But they are not badly off. The typical *ejido* member farms his own plot . . . , has a vegetable garden or some fruit trees in his back yard, and takes his family into Culiacán by bus once or twice a week to buy groceries and other needs. A few farmers have their own pickup trucks; many more have motorcycles. They are not rich, nor do they have much prospect of becoming so, but compared with their old life—a life still lived by many Mexican farmers—they are doing rather well. If this is not yet an affluent society, there are signs of affluence approaching. . . .

### Desert into Farmland

There are two kinds of farmers in Northwest Mexico— *ejido* members with plots of 10 to 14 hectares each, and small proprietors with holdings legally limited to 100 hectares within an irrigation district. Both have built their relative prosperity on the new infrastructure of improved road and rail service, electric power, and a highly efficient irrigation system. Together these basic facilities are enabling man to conquer what was, only a couple of decades ago, a vast stretch of inhospitable desert, punctuated here and there by small oases of farmland. These oases were made possible by water drawn from deep wells or pumped directly from the rivers by small, privately owned irrigation companies—a few going back to the 1920's. Gradually, the extension of irrigated land increased, but population growth was slow, and the Northwest remained isolated and backward. And, although in the hot climate the irrigated land produced abundantly, a serious salinity problem also developed, because the irrigation water contains some salt. If fields are not drained properly after irrigation, salt concentrations develop, and after a few growing seasons the land goes out of production, reverting to desert.

Furthermore, the very remoteness of the area was a problem. Access to markets was largely lacking. There was a railroad running from Nogales, on the Arizona border, to Guadalajara, in the center of the country, but it was notoriously inefficient. Washouts, derailments, unexplained delays were the rule, and the railroad became the butt of many jokes. The roadbed was incredibly rough, the rolling stock was ancient, passengers traveled at their peril. "Maintenance" was not a word in the vocabulary of the private company which operated it.

At least the railroad existed. Roads did not. A dirt track ran from north to south. Only adventurers tried it, and then only in the dry season. The one thousand kilometers from Culiacán to the United States border took ten days and a terrible toll in tire blowouts, breakdowns, and general driver frustration. The journey south to Guadalajara, was, if anything, worse, because the road eventually curved inland, twisting its way through rugged mountain country. Rivers and streams were crossed at fords, if at all, for after the rains they were impassable.

## Elements of Change

This was the situation of the Northwest for the first half of the twentieth century, changing little, economically depressed, stagnating. But about the time the farmers from

Michoacán moved to the north, the changes which were to transform the region began to occur. One was the establishment in 1947 of the Department of Hydraulic Resources—a cabinet-level government agency charged with planning and developing a system of irrigation for the whole of Mexico. Some of its earliest and most successful efforts have been in four of the river valleys of the Northwest—the Yaquí, the Mayo, the Fuerte, and the Culiacán.

Another harbinger of change was the highway, completed in 1952, giving the Northwest its first decent road communication with the outside world. Then, by 1955, the Mexican government had taken over the railroad, much to the relief of its private owners, and with the help of a $61 million loan from the World Bank, began to reconstruct the roadbed and to replace the antiquated locomotives and cars with modern equipment.

Throughout the 1950's another government agency—the Federal Electricity Commission—was also at work, and it too was receiving substantial World Bank financing. A thermal plant was built at Guaymas. As the Hydraulic Resources Department built its dams for storing irrigation water, the Federal Electricity Commission put in hydroelectric plants. Gradually old-fashioned and inefficient generating installations were retired, grids were interconnected, and lines were strung to towns and villages where previously the only electric power was provided by the generator for the local outdoor movie.

With the World Bank already involved in transport and power, in 1961 the Mexicans obtained the first of a series of loans for the irrigation program. The money earmarked for the Northwest—$15 million—helped to finance major extensions of irrigated land and also to reclaim fields contaminated by salt and lying idle. To do the work, the Department of Hydraulic Resources had assembled a corps of engineers and technicians, an elite body dedicated to the task at hand.

The irrigation districts of the Northwest have minor differences. More vegetables are grown in Culiacán, for example, than in Yaquí. There the big crop is wheat—the new, high-yielding strains developed in Mexico and now bringing about another agricultural revolution in Turkey, Pakistan, and India. Further north, in Mexicali, where last January [1968] the World Bank made another loan of $25 million to help to rehabilitate the Río Colorado district, the major crop is cotton. But the differences are less important than the similarities. For purpose of description, Culiacán can be considered typical.

On its way out from . . . [Culiacán], the road passes farm machinery distributors, fertilizer mixing plants, cotton gins, box-making plants, and storage facilities that bespeak big agriculture. There are great parking lots for refrigerated truck trailers, waiting to be loaded onto railroad flatcars, which go on their way to the produce dealers on the border in Nogales, who, in turn sell the fruits and vegetables to U.S. and Canadian buyers.

Traffic is constant along the highway, day and night. There are modern, air-conditioned buses well-loaded with passengers bound for Tijuana or Mexico City; trucks of all sizes, shapes, and description; farm machinery cautiously hugging the bank along the roadside. Today the highway has two lanes. Soon it will be a four-lane divided freeway, to link with a new road being extended southward to the fast-growing tropical resort, Puerto Vallarta.

Past the Culiacán airport, newly extended to accommodate medium-range jets, one turns off the paved highway onto a graded dirt road. On one side, a big, concrete-lined canal carries water from the man-made lake in the foothills to the east. Secondary canals branch off from the main one, bringing water to the fields. Land levelers are at work preparing one field; combines are harvesting in another. In still another, a hundred plastic siphons bring water from the secondary canals to rows of newly planted tomatoes. There is green everywhere, in a spectrum ranging from near-yellow to dark almost blue. The variety is immense; tomatoes, peppers, eggplant, squash, string beans, rice, lettuce, avocados, oranges and grapefruit, mangoes, corn, sorghum, and safflower, in a vast panorama stretching to the horizon. Deep, unlined ditches carry off the excess water, and help to save the land from salinity.

The packing sheds in the Culiacán district are out in the fields, near the source of supply. There were five of them in 1963. Today there are seventeen, all big operations, a central plant surrounded by housing for the workers. Like most company housing, it leaves much to be desired, although the economic condition of the workers is relatively good. . . .

### Reclaiming Salinified Land

Further westward toward the Gulf of California, the land changes. Much of it, once irrigated, is now out of production—covered by scrub desert plants and a scaly white crust. Here and there, a field stands under water. These are the salinified lands now being reclaimed or awaiting reclamation, effected by washing and draining. Depending on the seriousness of the problem, it can take as long as three or four years to reclaim contaminated fields. After agreeing with the owner on the program to be followed, the irrigation district surveys the land and brings in bulldozers to level it. Subsequently, dikes are built and the land is inundated. During the leaching process periodic tests are made to determine the progress of the decontamination program. Meanwhile, drainage canals are dug to carry off the irrigation water once the land is back in production, so that salinification will not recur. Landowners pay the irrigation district for its services, but the reclamation process has been slowed because farmers have been having difficulty in getting credit to finance the work. Medium-term and long-term loans for capital improvements are scarce in most developing countries. Mexico is no exception.

The farmers also get advice from the district on how to avoid future salinity. One way is to alternate fruit and vegetable crops, requiring intensive applications of water, with safflower, which requires less, and which allows the water table to drop. The district advisers are complemented by extension workers from the ministry of agriculture and experts from nearby government experiment stations. The irrigation districts also publish rather elaborate little magazines for circulation to their customers. They contain information about planting, harvesting, marketing, and the like. They have a question and answer column. They also publicize—somewhat in the manner of a rural chamber of commerce—the progress being made in the district in extending irrigation, reclaiming lands, and increasing yields. So far each year looks better than the one before.

## Social Change

Today, thanks to the projects in the river valleys of the Northwest and others throughout the country, Mexico grows enough to feed itself and to export in substantial quantity. A third of the crops are produced on that 13 per cent of cultivable area now under irrigation. The engineers of Hydraulic Resources are proud of their achievements; they have the visual evidence and the statistics to prove the importance of their contribution to Mexico. There may, after all, be enough food to take care of those 80 million Mexicans they talk about having by the year 2000, or maybe before.

But modernization is never a wholly positive story. On the irrigation projects themselves there have been delays and occasional mistakes. They are by and large well engineered and constructed, but there are instances in which concrete work has been faulty, in which maintenance has been poor, and in which the decontamination program of salt-logged lands has suffered delays. These are technical matters which are gradually being worked out.

One can question, too, some of the social side effects. With access to the outside world, and a money economy, some of the charms and traditional values of rural Mexico are disappearing. The village market, for example, is declining as an institution—as a social and communications center as well as a place to trade. Its replacement—the supermarket in town—could well be a supermarket anywhere. Colorful customs of dress are giving way to the styles featured by the apparel chain stores that now do a thriving business throughout the country. Regional differences disappear under the onslaught of television programs which are creating national tastes. . . .

## The Problem of Education

For the last year, a Mexican-American anthropologist on the faculty of the University of California has been living in the Los Mochis irrigation district, attempting to measure the impact of the project on the people of the *ejidos*. . . . Every *ejido* has its school, invariably the handsomest building in town. But most students stop at the sixth grade. They can read and write, add and subtract. They have an inkling of their country's past. They will most probably stay in the *ejido*, and their lives are not likely to change dramatically. Most of them will confine their reading, if they read at all, to pulp fiction and comic books. The anthropologist wondered aloud, without answering the question, whether a nation like Mexico can really afford universal education to the sixth grade while there is a severe shortage of medium-level technicians in almost every field. Perhaps the hard question of universal education at a low level versus training of needed technicians will someday have to be faced.

In the end, a development project must be judged by whether it has improved the condition and quality of life in a country or an area. In the economic sense, improvement can be easily measured. It is far more difficult, and far more subjective, to try to assess the social effects of change. Here we are in unknown territory. Who is to say for certain? There are disturbing aspects to Northwest Mexico. There are problems created by shifting values, and some of the imports from other cultures do not . . . [seem] either atractive or constructive. But the process of change will go on, because the Mexicans want it to go on. And life, on the whole, does really seem to have improved in that hot, sun-baked desert where water makes things grow.

# IV. DEVELOPMENT AND THE FUTURE

## EDITOR'S INTRODUCTION

What is taking place today throughout Africa, Asia, and Latin America has profound implications for the course of international affairs in the coming decades. As Professor Heilbroner explains in the first article of this section, what we are witnessing is a revolution of the most monumental proportions. There is a growing belief that something can be done about the poverty which shackles two thirds of the people on earth—and a growing impatience with the slow pace of progress.

In part, this is a struggle against the status quo which, according to Professor Heilbroner, the United States has generally attempted to defend, thus earning for itself the often violent opposition of revolutionaries throughout the underdeveloped world. Moreover, it has been suggested that only an authoritarian form of government can muster the force, energy, and ruthlessness required to ram through the necessary changes. All this presents a formidable set of challenges for U.S. foreign policy.

In the second article of this section, World Bank President Robert S. McNamara outlines his understanding of the kinds of assistance needed in the next decades. He sketches a program of action which will see the World Bank rapidly expanding its role as one of the prime stimulators of economic development. The following article presents a view of the role private capital could play in the development process. Except for investment in the extractive industries, however, private capital has not been taking advantage of the opportunities that exist in the developing world. The last article spells out how and where progress has been made in the past decade and offers a note of cautious optimism for the future.

## THE REVOLUTION OF RISING EXPECTATIONS [1]

Few Americans understand what the process of "econom-ic development" entails, or what the "revolution of rising expectations" really means. To most of us, development is merely a matter of money with which we assume economic advancement is bought. Unfortunately, money is the last, if not the least, step in the development sequence. For the long climb out of backwardness is not merely a matter of getting "richer." It is first and foremost a matter of changing an entire society in ways that must go to the roots of its ordinary life and that are bound to shake or topple its basic structure of power and prestige.

Actually, we have had a glimpse of the difficulties and dangers in trying to initiate "economic development" in the problems we have encountered at home in Harlem or Watts. We have learned, for example, that an enormous gulf must be bridged between the people who have to "develop" and those to whom the guidance of development is entrusted. The business and government leaders of Caracas or Rio or Calcutta have little or no contact with the dirty, ignorant, primitive people of the urban and rural slums of their coun-tries—in which live, however, not 10 or 20 per cent, but 70 or 80 per cent of the population. In turn, the inhabitants of the villages and urban slums regard the upper classes as rep-resentatives of a class whose only relation with themselves has been arrogant, exploitative, patronizing, or indifferent.

Second, both the slum and the underdeveloped areas smart under the constraints of absentee domination. We know of the resentment of the "radical" Negro against white-owned stores. Far greater is the resentment of the radical Asian, African, or Latin American against the foreign owner-ship of the main instruments of production in his country—the utilities, the manufacturing plants, railroads, planta-

[1] From "Making a Rational Foreign Policy Now," by Robert L. Heilbroner, professor of economics at the New School, New York. *Harper's Magazine.* 237: 64-75. S. '68. Copyright ©1968 by Harper's Magazine, Inc. Reprinted from the September, 1968 issue of *Harper's Magazine* by permission of the author.

tions, or oil fields. To be sure, one can answer that the supply of native entrepreneurship is small and that these foreign companies introduce capital and expertise that would otherwise be lacking. But they introduce as well a steady drain of earnings out of the country, and a basic orientation of business interest that is geared at least as much to the needs of the corporate home office as to the requirements of its host nation.

Last, we find another similarity between ghetto and backward land that may help us visualize the problems of economic development. This is the population problem that cuts away at both milieux. At home the rolls of relief mount steadily as the city poor produce more children than can be easily absorbed into society. Abroad, this disproportion between the rate of production of impoverished human beings and their social absorption takes on nightmarish dimensions. Each year we have watched Asia, the Near East, much of Africa and Latin America in a race between survival and starvation—a race that has already produced a devastating famine in India two years ago [in 1966]. By the year 2000 we shall have to run this race with twice as many human beings, and even with the brightest hopes for agricultural improvement, no one can face that prospect without flinching. President Ayub of Pakistan has put the threat succinctly: "In ten years' time, human beings will eat human beings in Pakistan."

### Ten Thousand a Day

These are some of the obstacles to economic development—obstacles that are obscured behind the bright slogan of "the revolution of rising expectations." They make it clear that much more is needed to bring improvement to the backward areas than money, just as much more is needed in our slums. At home, moreover, we are dealing with a minority that is in some kind of touch with a prevailing culture into which most of its members would, if they could, gladly enter. Abroad we are dealing with an ingrown, suspicious peasantry that has little or no understanding or acceptance of the modern ways that produce "loose" women and "disrespectful" children and a snubbing disregard of the wisdom of the village elders. So, too, at home we have an upper class that, however insulated from the slums, does not find its social position fundamentally incompatible with slum clearance. Abroad the clearance of the vast rural slums requires that its beneficiaries—the landed ruling class—give up their power and position to another ruling group. And finally, whereas the population problem at home exacerbates the problem of bringing economic improvement to the slum, abroad it renders this problem unmanageable.

Thus although Harlem and Watts give us some insights into India and Brazil, the problems of the latter are a thousandfold larger and more intractable than those at home. That is why the changes needed to bring development to the backward areas are so far-reaching that they are hard to describe as "reforms." Take, for example, the question of land reform—the breakup of the vast semifeudal land holdings that everyone, including our government, recognizes as incompatible with development. In Latin America, according to . . . an official in the Inter-American Committee on Agricultural Development in Washington, "There are families who own more land than is occupied by a number of sovereign states. . . . Statistically speaking, Latin America has the highest index of concentrated rural property in the world."

To urge land "reform" on such a society is tantamount to a visitor from Mars urging stock "reform" on us—telling us that great social benefits would accrue from breaking up the concentration of two thirds to three fourths of all privately owned corporate stock that lies in the hands of the top 2 per cent of American families. With how much enthusiasm would such a proposal be received in the United States and with how much carried out? Precisely the same response has greeted other proposals for land reform in Latin America.

But the trouble is not wholly that of upper classes who are unwilling to change the social system on which their power and prestige are based. There are other nations in the world—India is of course the prime example—where the terrible and persisting absence of necessary social change comes from the inability of mild men of good will to translate good intentions into effective deeds. Somehow a squabbling Congress, a nepotistic bureaucracy, and an overpowering atmosphere of futility have smothered every impetus to change, so that despite the intelligence and humane aspirations of the national leadership, we look with horror at the spectacle of the rotting poor who somehow cannot be housed or fed or put to work; at the world's largest collection of cattle, roaming through the country as an untouchable symbol of holiness and active agent of famine; at tens of thousands of still isolated villages where tens of millions of women remain in ignorance or fear of birth control.

It would be cruelly wrong to suggest that no progress has been made in the underdeveloped world. Compared with the past, giant strides have been taken. In Asia and Africa, millions of persons who, had you asked them to identify themselves a generation ago would have answered that they were so and so of such and such village, now answer that they are Pakistani, or Algerian, or whatever: the dangerous but necessary infection of self-conscious nationalism has become virtually pandemic. So, too, stirrings of modernization have made their way into the remote hamlets of Asia and Latin America alike: radios bring news of events in the capital city and the outer world; the cinema stirs imaginations; visitors from the cities bring new seeds which, cautiously tried, often bring better crops; there is talk of a school; a road is improved; an irrigation dam is built.

These changes are important and cumulative, but they must not be magnified out of proportion. First, were there no such changes, the Malthusian dilemma would by now have pushed even more millions below the starvation line (as it is, an estimated *ten thousand people a day* die of malnutrition in the underdeveloped areas). Second, the sum total of all these changes has not been enough to accelerate the rate of economic growth. In Latin America as a whole, gross national product has grown by a *smaller* percentage in each successive five-year period between 1950 and 1965. Virtually nowhere in Asia or the Near East or Africa does output per capita show a strong steady upward trend.* And last and most important of all, there is no evidence that the people themselves have been roused from their torpor, no release of energies from the great stagnant reservoir of humanity that is the basic repository of backwardness itself.

Instead what we see in virtually every corner of the underdeveloped world is a terrible changelessness that it seems impossible to affect. What we call "economic development" is in truth little more than a holding action that has succeeded only in building up the dikes just enough to keep the mounting population from washing away everything, not a movement that has invested life with a new quality. Change, insofar as it is being introduced, comes at a pace that is discouraging even to the most dedicated enthusiast. Thus we no longer hear the trumpets sound for the Alliance for Progress or the UN Development Decade. The outlook is for a continuation, no doubt with some small improvements, of the prevailing misery, filth, ill-health, and hunger for as long ahead as we can see.

This is not a "pessimistic" estimate. To be pessimistic would be to suggest a *worsening* of current trends—a cut in foreign aid, a petering out of the few birth-control programs that have begun, a collapse of foreign or domestic investment in the underdeveloped world because of growing unrest

---

* But what about the fabulous new agricultural techniques, such as the new seeds that yield up to twice the weight of output of present varieties? Our eager endorsement of technology as the cure for underdevelopment reveals all too clearly our failure to understand the social environment in which the process of change takes place. For the new seeds (in India and South America) are first used by the richer peasants. The poorer ones cannot afford to experiment for fear of starvation if the seed fails, or simply because, being poor, they are least "ready" for change. As a result the disparity in income between the upper stratum of peasants and the lowest widens. There is more food—but there is also more social misery.

there, a deterioration rather than an improvement in the caliber of governments. An optimistic appraisal would assume the contrary of these things. A realistic appraisal, I think, assumes that matters will go on much as they have gone on—a forecast that offers little room for rising expectations on our part.

To this general outlook for a continuation of the prevailing hopelessness of the backward world we must now add one final, all-important exception. It is that the sapping inertia of the underlying populace *has* been overcome within the last half-century in a very few nations.

One of these is of course Russia, whose leap into modernity has been the most extraordinarily rapid social transformation in history. Another, still more striking, is China. Even more hopeless, corrupt, and miserable than Russia, China was the source of endless horror stories of peasants eating mud when the crops failed, of the sale of daughters into prostitution to ward off starvation, of the subhuman degradation of the "coolie," the ricksha boy, the city homeless. China, in a word, was like India. But that too has changed. In China, we no longer find the homeless on the street, or forced prostitution, or children deliberately mutilated to become appealing beggars, although we still find all of these things in India. Nor do we find corruption in government, or an inability to distribute food supplies in bad times so as to provide a fair ration for all. More significant, we see an all-important redirection of Chinese life away from the endlessly static past to a new future—a redirection nowhere more dramatically expressed than in the spectacle of the youthful Red Guards indulging in the heretofore unthinkable action of defying their elders. To be sure, as the Red Guard also symbolizes, China is a nation in a paroxysm of change that has brought much that is ugly, cruel, and mean. And yet, before we condemn it for its very obvious evils, let every reader ask himself into which society he would take his chances as an anonymous human being today—India or China?

Last, there is the case of Cuba, never so impoverished as the other two, but also afflicted with the curses of underdevelopment in an uneducated rural proletariat and a corrupt city one. Every report from Cuba emphasizes that a tremendous effort is being made to eradicate these ills. Gambling and prostitution have disappeared in Havana. A great effort is being made in the countryside to bring education and agricultural reform. And if we may believe the testimony of articles both in *Look* magazine and in the New York *Times,* a new and genuine spirit of idealism and endeavor is to be found among the young.

I do not wish to rhapsodize over these countries in which life is still hard and harsh, and if one is an intellectual, often impossibly demeaning. Nor should one slight the important fact that China has not tackled its population problem and that Cuba has not yet built a well-functioning economy. Both nations may fail to bring about economic growth. Yet I would insist on one central achievement whose importance it is impossible to overstate. It is that these nations *have* succeeded in touching and bringing to life the deadened humanity that is the despair of the underdeveloped world. Even if they fail now, they have opened the way for a future assault that can succeed. One may fault the Communist nations on many grounds, not least that of morality—and on that score I will have more to say later—but one must also admit that they have brought hope, enthusiasm, and effort to the common people of their lands. *Of how many other backward nations can this be said?*

### Is Communism the Answer?

Does this imply that only a Communist government can bring about the revolution of rising expectations that is indeed the foundation on which development must rest?

This is not the conclusion I wish to urge. There are also a few non-Communist—although, please note, revolution-based—countries, Turkey and Mexico in particular, where at least the beginnings of a mass awakening have been carried out. Thus it is not communism, either as a system of philosophy or as a particular party, that makes the crucial difference, but a political movement that has the courage, conviction, and ruthless energy to carry through a program of modernization from top to bottom.

What is the galvanic force of such a movement? It lies first in the overthrow of an existing regime that is unable or unwilling to change the social order on which it rests. But that is only the initial stage in a developmental revolution, as contrasted with a purely political one. Next, such a movement must move with the full power of an authoritarian will to impose a program of change—often unwanted change —upon the very people in whose name the revolution has been waged—the underlying peasantry. Finally, it must bring to bear whatever economic compulsion is needed to mount the massive redeployments and concentrations of labor that will be needed to move the economy off dead center. . . .

### Chances for Slowing Down

Thus revolution, authoritarianism, and collectivism are often the *only* instruments by which essential social changes can be made. But having stated this as a generalization, let us now modify and soften the case as it applies to many individual nations. One need hardly say, for instance, that the prognosis for revolutionary change does not apply to Europe, where communism is an agent not at all for modernization but rather for political retrogression. But even in the backward world it would be wrong to deny the possibility of a more gradual and less traumatic evolution in some instances. In Africa, for example, many new nations are now undergoing the first trials of nationhood, including above all that of creating national consciousness and loyalties where only tribal affiliations existed before. These countries may experience their share of coups and turmoil, but it is unlikely that they will constitute fertile ground for mass revolutionary activity until a genuine national community has been forged.

And perhaps by that time a workable "African socialism" will permit the rigors of a revolutionary movement to be by-passed.

In Latin America the situation is much more revolution-prone, but even here some important nations may carry out their internal transformations without wholesale revolution. Argentina, with its relatively high standard of living and its low rate of population growth may be one such; Chile—provided that the reforms of President Frei are not blocked by the landholding and foreign interests—is another. As we have already said, Mexico, with a bloody revolution of national identity and foreign expropriation behind it, should be a third. In Asia, the long-run outlook is, perhaps least propitious of all, and yet even here a few nations may bring development to pass without resort to violent upheavals. . . .

Finally, taking the world as a whole there is always the possibility that a heroic effort to bring birth control to the masses, especially through the use of the plastic intrauterine device, might slow down the Malthusian timetable sufficiently to allow slower processes of change to work their way. Yet realism tells us that such a program will take decades to carry out; 97 per cent of the world's women do not use the pill or the plastic insert.

Last, when revolution comes, the leadership may spring from many sources other than Communist party membership. Angry and disillusioned army officers, idealistic middle-class intellectuals, even peasant guerrilla leaders may provide the nuclei that seed the clouds of potential disaffection. A movement that begins as a mere palace coup may find itself carried on its own momentum into a revolutionary trajectory. Thus revolution and communism are by no means synonymous, although it is undeniably true that Communists are working for and eager to lead a revolutionary thrust.

Whatever the leadership, however, it is clear that some sort of authoritarian nationalist socialism will be the vehicle of change. Whether or not this socialism will become Communist—that is, whether it will accept the dogmas and doc-

trines of Marxism and Maoism or seek active alliance with
Russia and China—depends on many events internal and external to the nation in question (including our own actions).
The nationalism that is so powerful a motive force in revolutions tends to drive the leadership away from communism
because of its danger of vassalage to a great state; the need
for moral support and technical advice may drive it toward
accepting or concocting some version of the Communist
catechism.

But it is important to realize that we should not expect
the attitude of a non-Communist revolutionary regime toward the United States to be very different from that of a
Communist one. For it is the unhappy fact that the United
States in recent years has thrown its support against *all* revolutions and provided its backing for *all* groups that have opposed revolutions, regardless of the merits of the one or the
demerits of the other—the scandal of our Dominican invasion,
our Guatemalan "success," and our Cuban "failure," our
backing of the militarist Branco in Brazil, and now our intervention in Vietnam all being instances in point. In the essential process of social surgery that must be performed if
many backward nations are to be brought to life, it is the
United States—for good reasons or bad—that delays the necessary stroke of the blade. That is why the revolution of economic development must become an anti-American revolution unless the United States changes its ways.

## In Place of Fortress America

But how to change our ways? How to cope with the forces
of economic development? To date we have lived with it in
a curiously schizophrenic way. On the one hand we have
been the leading agent of international assistance through
AID [Agency for International Development], the Peace
Corps, Food for Peace, etc. On the other hand we have been
the leader of the antirevolutionary forces of the world.

We have not, of course, meant to be schizophrenic. The
possible connection between revolution and development

has never been pointed out to us, particularly since the modernizing efforts of communism have been obscured by our steady emphasis on its repressive elements. Nor have we meant to oppose development in backing right-wing or center governments of Latin America or Asia. We continue to believe that development can take place gradually and peaceably, preferably with governments that "understand" the needs of the American business community. Hence our schizophrenia has ultimately been the price of self-deception —of unwillingness to confront the demanding process of development fearlessly or to acknowledge the inadequacies of our client governments to initiate deep and rapid social change. But now, if my prognosis is correct, this self-deception will be increasingly difficult to practice. As the pressures of revolutionary change build up, partly as a result of the bankruptcy of American policy in Vietnam, we shall have to face more squarely the harsh calculus of the developmental process. Indeed, the rise of the development revolution will force us to choose among one of three policies for the future.

The first of these is a continuation of our present policy. This will commit us to determined antirevolutionary activity, both political and military, wherever radical elements threaten to overthrow existing governments. I will not argue the consequences of this policy except to point out again that it presents the likelihood of a succession of Vietnam wars for the indefinite future.

An imaginable alternative is a *volte-face* in policy that would turn us away from all contact with the underdeveloped world. This would entail the creation of a fortress America, without diplomatic or economic—or direct military —contact with any revolutionary nations, defensively turned away from the inimical changes taking place in the underdeveloped continents. In the end this may be a policy to which we are forced to retreat, but it presents obvious dangers to the United States. An isolationist America, at bay in a revolutionary world, would bring forth the worst tendencies in this country, encouraging every superpatriot, fanning the fires of suspicion and fancied subversion, and submerging the humanitarian impulses that are the best side of the American national character.

The third policy is by far the most difficult to pursue, but is ultimately the only constructive course to follow. It is a policy of neutrality toward the revolutionary movement—a neutrality that ceases to oppose all revolutions as such, although not ceasing to differentiate between revolutionary regimes that we can actively support and those that we cannot. Such a policy does not ask us to endorse regimes that are bitterly anti-American in utterance or intolerable in behavior, nor does it prevent the political and military support of conservative government regimes threatened by subversion or submersion from neighboring states, *provided that these governments have the support of their people as a whole.* . . .

I need not point out the problems of steering such a course—of determining which revolutionary governments were acceptable and which governments under pressure warranted our support. But these problems would certainly be less than those encountered under a policy that recognized no revolutionary governments and that supported all anti-revolutionary ones. Indeed, if such a pragmatic and non-interventionist policy could be pursued in the future, a kind of victory could yet be snatched from the otherwise pointless and hideous sacrifices of the Vietnam war. For then it could be said some day that this war was for American foreign policy what the Great Depression was for domestic policy.

However difficult to carry out abroad, the real difficulties of such a policy of neutrality are apt to be encountered at home. For in changing our stance from one of belligerent opposition to one of neutrality, recognition, and selective aid, we would be sure to hear two frightening accusations from many groups in America.

The first of these would be that we were aiding and abetting an international aggressive movement whose rise would eventually engulf us. Frightening though it is, this accusation could be answered with some degree of assurance. For one thing, the alternative—military action abroad—has been revealed by the Vietnam war to be a policy that can bleed us white. For another, it is increasingly evident that communism is no more of a unified world force than capitalism ever was, and that the rise of many intensely nationalistic revolutionary states is much more apt to result in internecine warfare among themselves than in military action against us. . . . And last, there is simply the enormous disparity in industrial and military strength between America and Europe (and perhaps Russia on our side as well), and the populous but impoverished masses of the revolutionary world. A revolutionary world will assuredly be an extraordinarily dangerous, thin-skinned and rhetorically aggressive environment in which to make our way; but the specter of concerted military action of its impoverished governments against the rich nations an ocean's distance away is a fantasy that should not be difficult to destroy.

Not so easy to allay is another alarm that would accompany a policy of neutralism. It is that in acquiescing in the rise of Communist (or even non-Communist) regimes, we were condoning evil for expediency's sake.

This is not an accusation that can be readily countered by an appeal to reason. There is a strain of fundamentalism among sections of the American people that regards communism as the ultimate evil with which no compromise is imaginable and toward which no attitude but fear and loathing is possible.

It is true enough that communism has been a perpetrator of evil and it is all too likely that more evil will be committed in its name (or in whatever name is inscribed on the banners the revolutionists of development will carry). Yet if one cannot and should not seek to minimize the weight on that side of the scale of human suffering, one should also have the courage to pile up whatever weights belong on the other side.

This is not an operation we have carried out honestly. We tend to count carefully each corpse attributable to the terrorists, guerrillas, or avowed soldiers of revolutionary action, but to ignore the bodies of those who perish because of the actions of our own side, military or not. To whom, for example, should be charged the permanent and irreversible mental and physical stunting of Latin America's children that follows from an inability to alter the established social order? To whom shall we debit the grisly corpses, living and dead, in the streets of Bombay? In what account shall we enter the hunger of those who live within sight of the expensive restaurants of New Delhi or Lima or Hong Kong?

One does not know which way the scales of history would tilt if all the evils attributable to both sides were piled on their respective balances. But there is the uncomfortable suspicion that ours might not necessarily be the lighter side of the scale. What exists in most of the world beyond our borders is a condition of human indignity and degradation that verges on the unspeakable. If we are to set ourselves against a movement, however violent or cruel, that has demonstrated its ability to lead such men out of their misery for at least the first critical stage of the journey, we must at least offer something as good in its place. At this juncture it is the shameful fact that we have nothing as good, and worse than that, have ranged ourselves against nearly every movement that might have led men toward a better life, on the grounds of our opposition to communism. Now the question is whether America will take its ultimate stand on the side of humanitarianism or moralism, self-reliance or fear, open-mindedness or dogma. The challenge goes to the very core of this nation—its structure of power and economic interest, its capacity for reasoned discussion, its ultimate inarticulate values. It is not alone the life and death of anonymous multitudes that is weighed in the balance, but that of American conscience, as well.

## A DEVELOPMENT AGENCY AT WORK [2]

As the peoples of the world looked at the sixties—the United Nations' Development Decade—they felt a deep sense of frustration and failure. The rich countries felt that they had given billions of dollars without achieving much in the way of development; the poor countries felt that too little of the enormous increases in the wealth of the developed world had been diverted to help them rise out of the pit of poverty in which they have been engulfed for centuries past.

How far is this mood of frustration and failure justified by the events of the past decade? I have sought to find out the truth about this, but I confess, though there have been many voices only too anxious to answer my question, each with a panoply of statistics to prove its point, there is no agreed situation report, nor any clear joint strategy for the future.

There have been successes: many millions in aid have been forthcoming from the developed world, and as a result of that aid and of their own increased capacity to manage their affairs, the economic growth of the poorer countries has been stimulated. . . .

And yet . . . you know and I know that these cheerful statistics are cosmetics which conceal a far less cheerful picture in many countries. The oil-rich nations of the Middle East have prospered economically; so have some small states in East Asia. But for the nations of Africa and South Asia—nations with a population of over one billion—the average increase in national income is, at most, 3.5 per cent, and much of that is concentrated in the industrial areas while the peasant remains stuck in his immemorial poverty, living on the bare margin of subsistence.

[2] From "Text of Address by World Bank's New President," speech by Robert S. McNamara at the Bank's annual meeting, September 30, 1968. Text from the New York *Times*. p 58. O. 1, '68.

Casting its shadow over all this scene is the mushrooming cloud of the population explosion. If we take this into account, and look at the progress for human beings rather than nations, the growth figures appear even less acceptable.

### Income Growth Lags

The annual growth of per capita income in Latin America is less than 2 per cent, in East Asia only about 2 per cent, in Africa only 1 per cent, and in South Asia only about half a per cent. At these rates, a doubling of per capita income in East Asia would take nearly 35 years, in Latin America more than 40 years, in Africa almost 70 years and in South Asia nearly a century and a half. Even in the most progressive of these areas, the amount of improvement would be imperceptible to the average citizen from year to year.

Such a situation cries out for a greater and more urgent effort by the richer countries to assist economic growth in these poorer countries. It is clear they are financially capable of such action. During the Development Decade so far, they have added to their annual real incomes a sum of about $400 billion, an addition itself far greater than the total annual incomes of the underdeveloped countries of Asia, Africa and Latin America.

But I found, and I need hardly tell you this, that while the requirement for assistance was never higher, the will to provide it was never lower in many, though not all, of the countries which provide the bulk of economic aid.

And the disenchantment of the rich with the future of development aid was fed by performing deficiencies of many of the poorer nations. Blatant mismanagement of economies; diversion of scarce resources to wars of nationalism; perpetuation of discriminatory systems of social behavior and income distribution have been all too common in these countries. . . .

## Pearson Commission

In these circumstances, I turned to a suggestion which had been put forward by my predecessor, Mr. George Woods. . . . This was that we should establish a commission of men well versed in world affairs, and accustomed to influencing them, who would survey the past aid effort; seek out the lessons it can teach for the future; and then examine that future to see what needs to be done by rich and poor, developed and underdeveloped alike to promote the economic well-being of the great majority of mankind. . . . Mr. Lester B. Pearson, formerly prime minister of Canada, has agreed to lead such a survey. . . .

The Pearson Commission will be turning our eyes to the long future, marking out guidelines not just for a decade but for a whole generation of development that will carry us to the end of this century. But here are we now, living in 1968, with much that we can and must do today and tomorrow. It is already clear beyond contradiction that during the first four fifths of the development decade the income gap between the developed and the less-developed countries has increased, is increasing and ought to be diminished. But it is equally clear that the political will to foster development has weakened, is weakening further and needs desperately to be strengthened.

What can the . . . [World Bank] do in this situation? I have been determined on one thing: that the bank could and would act; it would not share in the general paralysis which was afflicting aid efforts in so many parts of the world. I do not believe that the bank can go it alone and do the job of development that needs to be done around the world by itself; but I do believe that it can provide leadership in the effort, and can show that it is not resources which are lacking—for the richer countries amongst them have resources in plenty—but what is lacking is the will to employ those resources on the development of the poorer nations.

*Plan for the Future*

We in the bank, therefore, set out to survey the next five years, to formulate a "development plan" for each developing nation, and to see what the bank group [the World Bank and its affiliated organizations] could invest if there were no constraint of funds, and the only limits on our activities were the capacity of our member countries to use our assistance effectively and to repay our loans on the terms on which they were lent.

As a result of this survey, we have concluded that a very substantial increase in bank group activities is desirable and possible. . . .

Let me begin by giving you some orders of magnitude: I believe that globally the bank group should during the next five years lend twice as much as during the past five years. This means that between now and 1973 the bank group would lend in total close to as much as it has lent since it began operations twenty-two years ago.

This is a change of such a degree that I feel it necessary to emphasize that it is not a change of kind. We believe that we can carry out these operations within the high standards of careful evaluation and sound financing that my predecessors have made synonymous with the name of the World Bank.

Our loans will be for projects as soundly based and appraised as ever in our history. However, more and more, in looking for projects to support we shall look for those which contribute most fundamentally to the development of the total national economy, seeking to break strangleholds on development; to find those growth opportunities that stimulate further growth. And our help will be directed to those poor nations which need it most.

This, I believe to be sound development financing, but it is not riskproof; nor do I believe that the utter avoidance of risks is the path of prudence or wisdom. I recently visited Indonesia where, for good reasons, the bank has never made a loan of any sort in the past. What I found was the sixth largest nation in the world, rich in natural resources, striving in the wake of the most terrible disasters, both economic and political, to set itself straight on the path to development. [See "Indonesia: Poor People in a Rich Land," Section II, above.—Ed.] Without external help it faces certain disaster; by giving help (as we have begun to do through the International Development Association and through the establishment of a permanent mission) we are running some risks. [The International Development Association is the branch of the World Bank which grants long-term low-interest loans to developing countries.—Ed.] . . .

But if we are to lend at double the level of the past, can we raise the money? I will not speak now about the soft-loan [low-interest] money which is raised by government contributions—you all know how essential these funds are—but about the money we raise by bond issues in the capital markets of the world. I am confident that the money is there, because I have confidence in the immense capacity of the economies of the developed world; no country need fear bankrupting itself because it plays its full part in development.

There are, of course, certain constraints through balance-of-payments difficulties, but I am fully aware that the balance-of-payments difficulty is a problem of balance among the rich economies and not of balance between those countries as a group and the rest of the world—very little of the money lent in aid stays in the developing countries, almost all of it returns quickly in payment for the goods purchased in the richer countries. It is our job in the World Bank to look at the world money markets as a whole, and see where there are surpluses, where there are reserves that can be tapped. Following this line we have gone to the Middle East, and successfully raised funds there, as well as in the more conventional markets of the world—in particular Germany and America.

As a result, in the first ninety days of this fiscal year [July 1968-June 1969] the World Bank has raised more funds by borrowing than in the whole of any single year in its history.

I have been stressing that in doubling the bank group's lending activities we are not departing from our high standards of investment policy. But I would not want you to think that our policy is simply "more of the same."

Our five-year prospect calls for considerable changes in the allocation of our resources, both to geographic areas and to economic sectors, to suit the considerably changed circumstances of today and tomorrow.

First as to area: in the past the bank group has tended to concentrate its effort on the South Asian subcontinent. Much has been achieved—the harnessing of the waters of the Indus River system for power and irrigation, for instance—and much remains to be achieved. I believe World Bank lending to Asia should rise substantially over the next five years. But it is not to Asia alone that our new effort will be directed. It is to Latin America and Africa as well, where in the past our activities have been less concentrated, and to some countries in great need of our help, such as Indonesia and the U.A.R. [United Arab Republic], where our past activities have been negligible.

In Latin America, I foresee our investment rate more than doubling in the next five years. But it is in Africa, just coming to the threshold of major investment for development, where the greatest expansion of our activities should take place. There, over the next five years, with effective collaboration from the African countries, we should increase our rate of investment threefold.

Further changes will flow from our shift to a greater emphasis on Africa and Latin America. The states of these two continents are smaller than the giants of Asia. There will be many more but smaller projects, demanding much more staff work per million dollars lent than in the past.

## Recruiting Drive

The work of the bank will also be increased because in many of the countries in which we will now be investing there is no well-established development plan or planning organization. We shall try, in conjunction with other sources of funds, to help these countries to develop plans and to adopt wise and appropriate policies for development—in some cases by establishing resident missions as we have done in Indonesia—but always remembering that it is their country, their economy, their culture and their aspirations which we seek to assist.

In particular, we will exert special efforts to right one upside-down aspect of bank group operations: the fact that many of our poorest members, despite their greater need, have had the least technical and financial assistance from the bank group. About ten of these have had no loans or credits at all. This is largely because of their inability to prepare projects for consideration. In these cases we will provide special assistance to improve economic performance and to identify and prepare projects acceptable for bank group financing. . . .

Not only should our lending double in volume and shift geographically, but we can foresee, as well, dramatic changes among sectors of investment. Great increases will occur in the sectors of education and agriculture.

## Education Outlays

Education is a relatively new field for the bank on which my predecessor . . . began to place increased emphasis. In recent years the bank has been seeking, uneasily but with a growing sense of urgency, to find its optimum role in this field.

We are aware of the immense numbers of illiterates in the developing world: about 30 per cent in Latin America, 60 per cent in Asia, 80 per cent in tropical Africa. We know, too, that education is relevant to all dimensions of development: it makes a more effective worker, a more creative manager, a better farmer, a more efficient administrator, a human being closer to self-fulfillment.

The need is clear, but it has been less clear how the bank's resources can be brought to bear on this labyrinthine problem. Now, after some years of collaboration with UNESCO [United Nations Educational, Scientific and Cultural Organization], we believe we see a way ahead for increasing bank investment which we hope will call forth further investment by the government of the developing country itself.

Our aims here will be to provide assistance where it will contribute most to economic development. This will mean emphasis on educational planning—the starting point for the whole process of educational improvement. It will mean assistance, particularly in teacher training, at all levels, from primary to university. It will mean expansion of our support for a variety of their educational activities, including the training of managers, entrepreneurs and of course of agriculturalists.

It is important to emphasize that education, normally one of the largest employers in any country, is one of the few industries which has not undergone a technological revolution. We must help to move it out of the handicraft stage. With the terrible and growing shortage of qualified teachers all over the developing world we must seek ways to make good teachers more productive. This will involve investment in textbooks, in audio-visual materials, and above all in the use of modern communications techniques (radio, film and television) for teaching purposes.

### Aid to Agriculture

To carry out this program we would hope over the next five years to increase our lending for education development at least threefold.

But the sector of greatest expansion in our five-year program is agriculture, which has for so long been the stepchild of development. Here again there has never been any doubt about its importance. About two thirds of the people of the developing world live on the soil, yet these countries have to import annually $4 billion of food from the industrialized nations. Even then their diet is so inadequate, in many cases, that they cannot do an effective day's work and, more ominous still, there is growing scientific evidence that the dietary deficiencies of the parents are passed as mental deficiencies to the children.

The need has stared us in the face for decades past. But how to help?

In the past, investment in agricultural improvement produced but a modest yield; the traditional seeds and plants did better with irrigation and fertilizer but the increase in yield was not dramatic. Now, as you know, as the result of research in the past twenty years, a breakthrough has taken place in the production of new strains of wheat and rice and other plants which can improve yields by three to five times [See "The Agricultural Revolution in Asia," Section III, above.—Ed.] What is more, these new strains are particularly sensitive to the input of water and fertilizer; badly managed they will produce little more than the traditional plants, but with correct management they will give the peasant an unprecedented crop.

Here is an opportunity where irrigation, fertilizer and peasant education can produce miracles in the sight of the beholder. The farmer himself in one short season can see the beneficial results of that scientific agriculture which has seemed so often in the past to be a will o' the wisp tempting him to innovation without benefit.

Our task now is to enable the peasant to make the most of this opportunity and we, with the continuing assistance of FAO [Food and Agriculture Organization], intend to do so at once and in good measure. Irrigation schemes, fertilizer plants, agricultural research and extension, the production of pesticides, agricultural machinery, storage facilities—with all of these we will press ahead in the immediate future. Indeed in the coming year we plan to process more than twice the value of agricultural loans as in the last, and our agricultural dollar loan volume over the next five years should quadruple.

There is an element of risk in all this, of course. The seeds were issued before all the tests had been completed; the resistance of the crops to local diseases or pests cannot yet be assured; the splendid harvests in India and Pakistan this year cannot all be attributed to the new seeds. But I have no doubt, though setbacks may lie ahead, that there has been an agricultural revolution as significant as any development since the industrial revolution. It is one that gives us a breathing spell in the race between man and his resources.

### Population Growth

This leads me to yet another area where the bank needs to take new initiatives—the control of population growth. This is a thorny subject which it would be very much more convenient to leave alone. But I cannot, because the World Bank is concerned above all with economic development, and the rapid growth of population is one of the greatest barriers to the economic growth and social well-being of our member states. . . .

As a development planner, I wish to deal only with the hard facts of population impact on economic growth. Recent studies show the crippling effect of a high rate of population increase on economic growth in any developing country. For example, take two typical developing countries with similar standards of living, each with a birth rate of 40 per thousand (this is the actual rate in India and Mexico) and estimate what would happen if the birth rate in one of those countries, in a period of twenty-five years, were to be halved to 20 per thousand, a rate still well above that in most developed countries. The country which lowered its population growth would raise its standard of living 40 per cent above the other country in a single generation.

In terms of the gap between rich countries and poor, these studies show that more than anything else it is the population explosion which, by holding back the advancement of the poor, is blowing apart the rich and the poor and widening the already dangerous gap between them.

## THE WORLD-WIDE OPPORTUNITY FOR PRIVATE CAPITAL [3]

It is doubly unfortunate that the flow of capital from the richer countries should have stagnated at a time when the ability of the poorer countries to use such capital has increased impressively. There was a time not so long ago when people said that it was not easy to find sound and well-conceived projects in the developing countries that were worth financing; the suggestion was implicit that the money was there but the projects were not. The situation today is very different. Now the projects are there, but the money is not. The World Bank's estimates suggest that the developing countries have reached the stage where they are in a position to use, efficiently and profitably, . . . [about] $3-4 billion more of capital each year than they are getting. That is to say, they are at present receiving about $9 billion of capital annually; but they are able to use—and, I emphasize, the word *use* here means "use efficiently and profitably"—more than $12-13 billion each year.

### Vast Scope for Investment

This gap of $3-4 billion gives some idea of the vast scope for useful investment in the developing countries today. Admittedly, not all of the $3-4 billion is needed for projects which private investors normally could or would like to finance. Much of it is needed for improving the infrastructure of an economy, which private enterprise has traditionally,

[3] From article by Abderrahman Tazi, World Bank official and former Moroccan diplomat. *Finance and Development* (International Monetary Fund and World Bank). 5:13-17. S. '68.

and for understandable reasons, been reluctant to finance directly. Such projects may relate to highways, ports, railroads, or agriculture and education. . . . But even if projects to improve the infrastructure of an economy are excluded from the total of $3-4 billion, there is enough left for private investors to do—in fields with which they are fully familiar and in which they could operate much more effectively. The opportunities clearly are vast, and . . . the flow of private foreign capital to the developing countries could and should be increased rapidly. But before it is, what is required first is a fundamental change in outlook and attitudes. By this I mean that the task of international economic development today is not one which can be left to governments or international institutions alone. It is one in which private enterprise has to accept its share—and the share has to be much larger than it has been so far. Private enterprise has the vigor, the resourcefulness, the flexibility, and the resiliency which few other forms of organization can claim to have.

The great merit of private enterprise, and especially foreign private enterprise, is that it does not simply provide the money. Along with the money, it provides technical expertise, managerial skills, and marketing know-how—assets which are as scarce in developing countries as capital itself, and which are no less essential for success. More and more developing countries have recognized the fact, and have striven to atract the foreign capital they urgently need. But the results so far have been disappointing; international private investment still flows mainly to the developed countries rather than to the developing ones.

### Steps Already Taken

In recent years, the developing countries have taken a number of important steps to stimulate the inflow of foreign private capital. Many of them have set up investment promotion centers as a symbol of their intention. An outstanding example is Morocco, which in July 1967 established the Centre d'Accueil et d'Orientation des Investisseurs [Welcome and Orientation Center for Investors]. Although the center is young, it has already begun to act as an intermediary between foreign private investors and the government with regard to specific investment proposals. The center is thus helping to underline the enormous potential for economic growth in Morocco—a country which, because of its geographical position, could become a major source of manufactured supplies for the rapidly growing economies of the European Common Market [composed of France, West Germany, Italy, Belgium, the Netherlands, and Luxembourg.— Ed.].

In several instances, the governments of the poorer countries have given assurances, implicit or explicit, of fair treatment to foreign private investors. In other instances, insurance has been formally offered against the risks of nationalization or expropriation. Under the World Bank's auspices, the Centre for the Settlement of Investment Disputes has been organized to provide facilities for settling investment disputes by voluntary recourse to conciliation or arbitration, or both. Another proposal now being considered relates to the setting up of an International Investment Insurance Agency which would provide essentially the same protection to private foreign investors against noncommercial risks that is presently available under certain individual national programs. These . . . are important steps toward developing a sense of security and confidence in the minds of private foreign investors. But they have made no impact on the actual flow of private capital to the developing countries so far.

In the circumstances, it is often hard to be sure what range of assurances, guarantees, and legal and institutional paraphernalia will give private investors the confidence they look upon as an essential precondition for making their investments. The political instability seen in many developing countries—or, for that matter, in many developed ones—is understandably a source of concern to potential investors. But one could say that there is no complete and permanent assurance of political stability to be found anywhere on this troubled earth of ours. In some countries, political unrest takes the form of what is popularly described as the crisis of the cities, or a racial problem, or the revolt of youth. In others, it may take forms that are more spectacular but not always more serious. On the long view, it is hard to be sure which types of unrest are likely to prove more damaging to economic progress.

## Poverty and Wealth

But at least one thing can be said: the political troubles of the less-developed countries are often simply a reflection of their economic frustration in the midst of abysmal poverty. In other words, their political instability can be moderated only by economic progress—of the sort which it is the duty of private enterprise to promote in its own unique ways. Even in the midst of the unrivaled affluence of the United States, one does not have to look far to notice that the underfed and the underprivileged represent the single most important threat to orderly progress in future years. The problems of the poor and underprivileged, against which the United States is battling—with its great wealth, genius, and vigor—are not essentially different from the problems against which the Third World is battling—in the face of far more formidable handicaps. It may not be too great an oversimplification to say that the politico-economic problems of the Third World are in many ways the politico-economic problems of the U.S. poor—but multiplied in magnitude a thousand times.

## True Role of Private Enterprise

Some hardheaded businessmen might at this point turn round and say that the poor and the underprivileged are not their concern; as businessmen, their first concern is with their duty to their stockholders, through the security and profitability of the investments they make. They might go on to argue that private capital is scarce; the intangible assets which it brings with it, in the form of enterprise, know-how, and efficiency, are even more scarce. Therefore, it is up to the developing countries to recognize the scarcity value of these assets and to pay the price asked for them, since private capital will go only where the biggest profits are. But I suggest that the responsible sectors of private enterprise simply do not go where profits are biggest. The truth is that private enterprise goes where the profits, which are essential to its survival, can be combined with a recognition of social responsibility. . . .

The closer identification of private enterprise with the broader aims of the nation and the society has been one of the outstanding developments of the twentieth century in the richer countries. In many of the developing countries, unfortunately, this identification is still lacking. It is true that quite often the developing countries themselves, or their leaders, are to blame; in newly independent nations, for instance, fears and prejudices are apt to persist as a hangover from a colonial era in which the record of private enterprise may not have been uniformly creditable. But even in dealing with countries where such fears and prejudices never existed, or where they have receded into the shadows of the forgotten past, the approach of private enterprise has been marked by reluctance and nervousness. One is reminded of countries like Ghana and Indonesia which, following a series of political upheavals some time ago, have begun to welcome foreign private enterprise with open arms. Yet the response they have received, in terms of positive investment decisions, has been extremely disappointing. In other words, the opportunities are there—and they are growing—but there are disturbing signs that they are going to be missed.

### Supplying the Food

The sort of opportunities I particularly have in mind are those arising from the desperate shortage of food in developing countries—a shortage which threatens to become even more desperate in the coming years. Recognizing the seriousness of the threat, many of the poorer countries are becoming increasingly aware of the need to revitalize and strengthen their agriculture. A vast demand is arising for the myriad inputs which private industry is in a position to manufacture and supply. In meeting this demand, businessmen from the developed countries have the ability to make a uniquely important contribution—with as great a benefit to themselves as to the countries they invest in. They know from experience that the astonishing agricultural progress achieved by their own countries since World War II, or even earlier, would simply not have been possible if private industry had not joined in the endeavor. Not only did industry help to provide agricultural inputs like fertilizers, pesticides, better implements, new machinery, and irrigation equipment, it also did much to promote the use of more scientific techniques of cultivation. No less important, it carried to the agricultural sector its own enormous fund of experience of such problems as distribution, marketing, and storage. It played the major role in transforming agriculture into an industry, and thereby giving it the strength and the viability necessary for rapid economic growth.

The problems of agricultural progress in the developing countries today are not very different. In many ways, they are precisely the problems which private industry has handled so superbly in the richer countries in earlier years. The developing countries now represent a vast potential market not only for the agricultural inputs but also for the techniques and experience which many private investors in the richer countries are so well equipped to offer.

Nor is it in agriculture alone that the developing countries present a whole new world of opportunity. Looking a little further ahead, as research progresses and new techniques emerge, similar opportunities are likely to arise in dealing with the parallel, but far more challenging, problem of population growth. Private industry in the developed countries is rapidly accumulating the fund of scientific resources and research experience that will be required for a concerted attack on this problem. What is more, it promises soon to have the know-how and the business acumen necessary for putting family-planning programs on a strong and commercially viable basis. The opportunities, therefore, are there; and they exist in the fields which the developing countries themselves have begun to recognize as of top economic priority. What is lacking is an awareness of the opportunities and their importance to the business world of tomorrow.

## Changing Attitudes

The point about the new opportunities arising in the priority sectors should be emphasized for at least one good reason. Even in developing countries, where the climate for foreign private investment is considered less favorable than it should be, foreign-owned enterprises which have managed to identify their activities with the country's own list of priorities have done far better than the rest. It is true that doubts and differences of opinion have arisen from time to time even among these types of enterprise. It is also true that the doubts and differences—whether economic, political, or simply psychological in origin—have not always been overcome easily or quickly. But the basic point remains: the more closely an enterprise has attuned its activities to the nation's own sense of priorities—and attuned it in fact instead of merely in newspaper advertisements—the more secure and profitable its operations have been.

The attuning cannot be left to come about simply as an accident of circumstance. The precondition for it is confidence and understanding, both of which take time to grow. Therefore, instead of the take-it-or-leave-it attitude which is still far too common today in investment negotiations, the need is for an informed and continuing dialogue between investors and the developing countries. Investors have sometimes been heard to complain that the stamina of developing countries, and especially of their governments, for dialogues without results is inexhaustible. This may well be true of some. But, on the other side, the complaint is no less frequent that foreign investors sometimes prescribe impossible conditions for making their investments. There have been instances where they have sought terms which would give them an effective monopoly over markets, or would bring them exorbitant profits in other ways. By such means they have sought to protect themselves not only against non-commercial risks but also against commercial ones.

Against this background, it seems that certain fundamental changes in investors' outlook and attitudes are required. Unfortunately, these changes are apt to occur even more slowly than changes in governments' policies. The recent experience of countries like Ghana and Indonesia support this impression. So might the fact that the positive incentives which the governments of many of the richer countries have offered for private investment in the developing countries have taken a long time to mature into a recognizable increase in the flow of foreign private capital. So might the fact that the measures which the poorer countries have taken to attract foreign private capital have yielded results rather slowly, even in countries which have no long history of hostility toward such capital to live down.

## A Time for Action

Clearly, the intangibles in the relationship between foreign private investors and the developing countries—intangibles such as confidence and understanding—are often as important as the tangibles, such as the prospective profitability of the operations or the likely size of the markets. But that is all the more reason why an informed and constructive debate on the role of foreign private capital and its usefulness and appropriate spheres of activity should be encouraged.

It is unfortunate that, among potential investors, debates on the proper role of foreign private capital often create misunderstanding; the impression arises, rightly or wrongly, that the debate itself is evidence of hostility. In fact, however, investors have little to lose from such an exchange; they have an excellent case to present, and they have every reason to welcome the opportunity to present it forcefully.

What is more, only in this way is it possible to clarify issues and define policies in the detail in which investors would want them clarified and defined. The proper role of foreign private capital in a developing country is as legitimate a subject as any for democratic debate; it is only through such a debate that the fog of suspicion, doubt, and hostility can be lifted. . . .

The present is a particularly opportune moment for a major collaborative effort to begin. In recent years, more and more of the developing countries have started to recognize the great contribution which private enterprise, especially foreign private enterprise, can make to their economic progress. The time may not be far off when private enterprise, in turn, begins to realize how impressively the scope for investment in the developing countries has grown in recent years—and, with the new emphasis on agricultural development, how rapidly it is likely to grow in the future. In this situation lie the seeds for closer collaboration between foreign private investors and the developing countries—for collaboration of a kind that could bring immeasurable benefits to both.

## THE REALITY OF PROGRESS [4]

Given the overwhelming nature of the . . . barriers to development, it is perhaps astonishing that the low-income countries should have made as much progress in this decade as they have. If the experience of the 1960's tells us anything, it is that economic progress is possible in almost any region of Africa, Asia, and Latin America—given a reasonable degree of internal stability, a government eager for modernization, a leadership willing to take the disciplined steps necessary for progress, a tax system which invites incentive, fiscal policies which encourage savings and investment and, if the country is fortunate, large amounts of assistance in those

[4] From address by Irwin Isenberg, United Nations Development Program officer, delivered at the University of Wisconsin, July 17, 1968. Mimeographed.

critical areas where it is not able to marshal the requisite resources by itself. This is a formidable list of conditions, but they have already been realized in a number of countries. Special mention should be made of the fact that there is a high correlation between those countries whose development efforts have met with success and those which have received unusually large amounts of external assistance. This assistance might come from bilateral or multilateral sources or even from such external earners of foreign exchange as tourism.

## National Achievements

Our own southern neighbor, Mexico, is moving ahead with giant strides. In the last seven years, the average income of its citizens has grown by more than 50 per cent and the domestic consumption of goods by almost the same amount. In this time period, the value of Mexico's manufactured goods has increased by two thirds and the yield per acre of some of the important agricultural crops by more than one half.

Pakistan's progress, considering its far greater poverty, is even more impressive. Since 1950, Pakistan's gross national product has virtually doubled; during the present decade its economic growth rate has topped 5 per cent annually compared with a less than 3 per cent annual growth in population. In 1968, Pakistan harvested a record wheat crop and there was hope that the country would be able to achieve virtual self-sufficiency in agricultural production by 1975 or soon thereafter.

Since 1960, the Ivory Coast has invested some $700 million in domestic development, more than half of which came from the private sector of the economy. This investment has paid handsome dividends—with per capita income rising by an estimated average of some 8 to 10 per cent annually.

Even granting that such statistics should not be considered an exact measure of success, they may at least be properly viewed as broad indicators of progress. Consider the example of India—a country where population problems are of overwhelming proportions, where slums are of such appalling horror as to be literally beyond the imagination of almost any American who has not actually seen them, where several hundred million people are illiterate, where every development issue seems to be present in larger than life size. [See "Can India Survive Calcutta? in Section II, above.—Ed.] In the last fifteen years, as United States Ambassador Chester Bowles has written, this same India has increased its steel production sevenfold, its electric power capacity fivefold, its school population fourfold and its cultivated acreage nearly twofold. In the course of this progress, some 30 million jobs have been created.

The basic achievements [Ambassador Bowles says] have created a solid base for further development; indeed many American and Indian economists are persuaded that with normal rains and continuing foreign aid, India may become self-sufficient in food grain by 1972 and able to do without foreign governmental assistance by 1977.

It is well known that Greece, Spain, Israel, Lebanon, and Taiwan made such substantial progress in the 1950's and 1960's that they were able to "graduate" from the U.S. program of economic assistance. The progress of such countries as Brazil, Chile, South Korea, Tunisia, and Turkey has been greater in some economic sectors than even the most optimistic reports had predicted. After accounting for inflationary price increases, Brazil, for instance, has more than doubled its gross national product and national income in the last two decades. Twelve countries—among them Mexico, the Philippines, Sudan, Tanzania, and Thailand—have increased their average annual agricultural yields over sustained periods at a rate higher than that ever achieved by the developed countries over a similar span of years. And in industry, the developing countries are estimated to have achieved an average annual growth rate of almost 7 per cent in the decade prior to 1966.

*Success in Perspective*

But these achievements, as significant as they are, should be viewed in their proper context. Many of the statistics relating to low-income country economies tend to distort the degree of progress because, with a low base figure, any increase may result in a sizable percentage rise. Furthermore, there are many countries whose economies have recorded only modest gains and which have made very little headway in view of rising populations. On balance, the results thus far obtained are no more than first steps—and, though perhaps spectacular in themselves, rather modest when compared to need.

The fact that steel production or gross national product has increased does not necessarily mean that the man in the street has realized any benefit in relation to his own living standard. In fact, despite the creation of those 30 million jobs in India, the country probably has more unemployed people now than it had in 1955. Throughout much of the world, per capita annual income is at a subsistence level. In terms of food, more than half the world's population still suffers from an improper diet. . . . In terms of education and housing, the low-income countries may not be much better off now than they were a decade ago because government programs can scarcely keep up with the new demands caused by increasing population, let alone fill the backlog of unsatisfied needs. Entire families sleep on the streets in Asia, while millions of others in Africa and Latin America live in abysmal poverty. Even the rather more satisfactory growth in the manufacturing sector leaves much to be desired. This growth could not satisfy demand or provide enough employment opportunities and was, by itself, not large enough to generate a 5 per cent increase in per capita income.

Nevertheless, as serious a picture as these statements reflect, it is plainly unwarranted to believe that progress is impossible or that what has already been accomplished in the 1960's is of small consequence. What some of the less-developed nations have achieved is nothing short of astonishing, particularly in view of the tremendous difficulties and pressures under which they have been working.

## Availability of Resources

One notion which is widely—and erroneously—held is that many countries lack the physical and human resources to provide a sound basis for development. Actually, quite the contrary is true. In the past twenty years, many of the previously unsurveyed areas of the world have been studied and mapped. The results have been surprising. Our planet is far richer in resources than almost anyone had imagined. Large exploitable mineral resources have been discovered in numerous countries: coal in Colombia and Pakistan, copper in Argentina and Thailand, oil in Libya and Algeria, iron ore in Mexico and Chile, gold and chromite in Senegal. This is only a small sampling.

Forest inventories have cataloged enormous stands of timber in Mexico, Honduras, and other countries. In some instances, national governments were unaware of the extent of their lumber resources. River surveys on all continents have indicated the potential for virtually limitless power development and for vast increases in the acreage of irrigated agriculture. Development of such waters as the Mekong River in Asia or the Senegal and Niger Rivers in Africa would stimulate tremendous improvements in living standards for large areas. Fisheries could be developed, new land irrigated and cultivated, transportation improved, industry expanded, and income raised.

In one region of Syria, underground reservoirs, which could help in the cultivation of some 250,000 acres of presently unproductive land, have been located. Large underground water supplies have also been found in Israel and other countries. Soil studies have identified many fertile areas for future or more intensive agricultural cultivation. In Colombia, a survey carried out by the United Nations Development Program and the Food and Agriculture Organization has identified more than 30 million acres of low-yield land whose output could be greatly increased by more intensive farming methods, irrigation, and flood prevention measures. The list of unexploited or underexploited resources could be lengthened indefinitely. And it should be remembered that some countries such as Israel and Taiwan have been able to make rapid progress without having large amounts of natural resources.

But any discussion on the availability of resources should be qualified. There are a number of countries which have few known natural resources and whose generally low level of education prevents the population from developing skills to overcome nature's omission. Physical resources may not be lacking in many other low-income countries, but the real bottleneck is the underdevelopment of the human resources necessary to develop this potential. A substantial amount of investment capital—much more than the low-income countries are capable of allocating and much more than they are receiving from all public or private external sources—would be necessary to exploit these human resources which, in turn, would enable physical resources to be used more productively.

Many of the mineral deposits cannot be worked until roads and railways from the site to a processing or shipping point are built. The proper utilization of forest resources requires costly pulp, paper, and timber complexes as well as skilled workers and technicians. To realize hydropower potential is no less a costly process. To enlarge, appreciably, land areas under cultivation or to initiate more intensive farming measures is an expensive, time consuming, and difficult job. A development project not only requires capital and labor; it also requires a body of administrators, managers, engineers, and other professionals—all of whom are in extremely short supply in the low-income countries and not enough of whom can be supplied from abroad through bilateral or multilateral assistance programs.

## Making Development Work

Yet, when a country is able to marshal adequate support —either internally or with external help—for its development efforts, the results are often dramatic. Certainly no country appeared to be in worse shape than Libya when it gained independence in 1951. With a per capita income of $35 annually, it may well have been the poorest self-governing territory in the world at the time. With desert covering some 97 per cent of its 680,000 square miles and with more than 85 per cent of its people illiterate, its future hardly looked promising.

But thanks to the discovery of oil in 1957, and with the help of bilateral assistance from the United States, Britain, France, Italy, Turkey, and other countries, as well as multilateral assistance from the United Nations, the future has become brighter for Libya. Today, its per capita income is estimated at more than $400 annually—though this money is, of course, unevenly distributed throughout the population. Nevertheless, by law the government must devote about 70 per cent of its oil revenue—which amounted to some $1 billion in 1967—to development projects. In the course of a five-year plan which ended in 1967, numerous public buildings were constructed, school and hospital systems were expanded, efforts were made to diversify the economy and social development projects were begun. The economy is by no means robust, nor is Libya—despite its oil—a rich country. But the changes which have occurred in this decade may have been greater and more far-reaching than the sum of the changes of the last five hundred years.

Malawi provides another example. It is a landlocked nation in the southern part of the African continent. Malawi has no known exploitable mineral deposits and its economy is based almost entirely on agriculture. Even though the land is fertile, much of the agriculture is of a subsistence nature and large numbers of people must supplement family income by traveling to neighboring countries to find work. Several years ago, an internationally assisted project to assess land and water resources in one region of the country got under way. Requests were eventually prepared asking for international financing for the long-range improvement of agriculture. In early 1968, the International Development Association approved long-term, low-interest credits totaling nearly $10 million to expand agricultural extension services, introduce soil conservation practices, build secondary roads, improve water supplies, and open new avenues of agricultural credit. This loan is expected to help Malawi achieve a tenfold increase in its marketable surplus of maize, a staple food, and a threefold increase in the cotton crop.

Brazil offers one more example of what may be possible when sufficient financial support for the development of natural resources can be found. The country's south-central region is its most developed area industrially and agriculturally. The district's water power resources are enormous, but less than 10 per cent of the estimated potential is being utilized. With United Nations and other multilateral assistance, rivers in the region were surveyed, preliminary designs and cost estimates of potential hydropower sites were prepared, power market surveys made and a fifteen-year development program drawn up. On the basis of this information, the World Bank gave Brazil a $229 million loan for power development. The Brazilian government and private domestic sources invested more than $100 million of their own funds for the same purpose, while the United States and West Germany aided with smaller amounts. When the necessary construction work is completed, Brazil will be in a position to utilize more of its power potential—and this in turn will spur the further development of industry and agriculture. As a result of this and a large number of additional development projects, Brazil may enter the ranks of the wealthier industrialized countries by the end of the century. . . .

The low-income countries are also rich in human potential. Although every underdeveloped country suffers from crippling personnel shortages in many job categories, the lessons of the past decade have taught that nationals every-where are ready and eager to learn—if given the chance. In 1960, India began a long-range and complex project to ex-pand its national vocational training network for industrial trades. Its aim was to establish an organized system of guid-ance, planning, and supervision for apprenticeship training in industries so that up to 100,000 students could be receiving instruction at any one time and so that a steady flow of skilled workers could be made available to industry. The United Nations Development Programme and the Interna-tional Labour Organisation aided this project by helping India train the large amount of instructors needed to fulfill its goal. By 1968, instructor-training institutes were turning out some two thousand teachers during each school year. The teachers were then being sent to staff the national and state network of trade schools. . . .

Such examples are plentiful, but as yet they represent only drops of effort in a sea of need. As already stressed, the great tragedy of underdevelopment lies in the poverty of opportunity and the continued waste of human potential which is not able to be nourished because of the scarcity of funds and facilities. However, given a greater amount of re-sources channeled into development purposes and greater efforts to use these resources in the most effective manner possible, there is good reason to believe that more adequate rates of progress can be achieved.

# BIBLIOGRAPHY

An asterisk (*) preceding a reference indicates that the article or a part of it has been reprinted in this book.

## BOOKS, PAMPHLETS, AND DOCUMENTS

Alexander, R. J. A primer of economic development. Macmillan. '62.

American Assembly. Overcoming world hunger; report of the 34th American Assembly, October 31-November 3, 1968, Harriman, New York. Prentice-Hall. '69.

Balassa, Bela. Trade prospects for developing countries. Irwin. '64.

Black, C. E. The dynamics of modernization: a study in comparative history. Harper. '66.

Black, L. D. The strategy of foreign aid. Van Nostrand. '68.

Burnet, Mary. ABC of literacy. UNESCO. '65.

Currie, L. B. Obstacles to development. Michigan State University Press. '67.

*Foreign Policy Association. Great decisions 1969. The Association. 345 E. 46th St. New York 10017. '69.
    *Reprinted in this book*: Fact Sheet no 3. Africa, Asia and the Development Decade. p 25-7.

Freeman, O. L. World without hunger. Praeger. '68.

Friedmann, W. G. and others. International financial aid. Columbia University Press. '66.

Geiger, Theodore. The conflicted relationship: the West and the transformation of Asia, Africa and Latin America. McGraw. '67.

Hambidge, Gove, ed. Dynamics of development. Praeger. '64.

Hauser, P. M. ed. The population dilemma. Prentice-Hall. '63.

*Hauser, P. M. World population problems. (Headline Series no 174) Foreign Policy Association. 345 E. 46th St. New York 10017. D. '65.

Hazelwood, Arthur, ed. African integration and disintegration. Oxford University Press. '68.

Heilbroner, R. L. The great ascent; the struggle for economic development in our time. Harper. '63.
    *Excerpt*. Reader's Digest. 82:21+. F. '63. What it's like to be underdeveloped.

Higgins, Benjamin. Economic development: principles, problems, and politics. Norton. '68.

Hirschman, A. O. The strategy of economic development. Yale University Press. '58.

Hoffman, P. G. One hundred countries, one and one quarter billion people: how to speed their economic growth, and ours, in the 1960's. Albert and Mary Lasker Foundation. Washington, D.C. '60.

Hoffman, P. G. World without want. Harper. '62.

*Horowitz, David. Hemispheres north & south: economic disparity among nations. Johns Hopkins Press. '66.
    Reprinted in this book: The have and the have-nots. p 3-13.

*Isenberg, Irwin. The reality of progress; address at University of Wisconsin, July 17, 1968. mimeo.
    Not available for distribution.

Johnson, D. G. The struggle against world hunger. (Headline Series no 184) Foreign Policy Association. 345 E. 46th St. New York 10017. Ag. '67.

Jones, J. M. The United Nations at work: developing land, forests, ocean, and people. Pergamon Press. '65.

Joyce, J. A. Decade of development: the challenge of the underdeveloped nations. Coward-McCann. '67.

Kaplan, J. J. The challenge of foreign aid: policies, problems and possibilities. Praeger. '67.

Kerr, M. H. The Middle East Conflict. (Headline Series no 191) Foreign Policy Association. 345 E. 46th St. New York 10017. O. '68.

Laufer, Leopold. Israel & the developing countries; new approaches to cooperation. Twentieth Century Fund. '67.

Lewis, J. P. Quiet crisis in India; economic development and American policy. Brookings Institution. 1775 Massachusetts Ave. N.W. Washington, D.C. 20036. '62.

McGovern, G. S. War against want. Walker. '64.

Meier, G. M. International trade and development. Harper. '63.

Mikesell, R. F. The economics of foreign aid. Aldine. '68.

Millikan, M. F. and Blackmer, D. L. M., eds. The emerging nations; their growth and U.S. policy. Little. '61.

Montgomery, J. D. Foreign aid in international politics. Prentice-Hall. '67.

Montgomery, J. D. The politics of foreign aid. Praeger. '62.

Moomaw, I. W. The challenge of hunger; a program for more effective foreign aid. Praeger. '66.

Mountjoy, A. B. Industrialization and under-developed countries. Hillary House. '63.

Myrdal, Gunnar. Asian drama: an inquiry into the poverty of nations. 3v. Pantheon. '68.

Myrdal, Gunnar. An international economy; problems and prospects. Harper. '56.

Nair, Kusum. Blossoms in the dust: the human factor in Indian development. Praeger. '62.

Paddock, William, and Paddock, Paul. Famine—1975! Little. '67.

Pincus, John, ed. Reshaping the world economy: rich countries and poor. Prentice-Hall. '68.

Pincus, John. Trade, aid and development: the rich and poor nations. McGraw. '67.

Prebisch, Raúl. Towards a global strategy of development. United Nations. '68.

*Rivkin, Arnold. The new states of Africa. (Headline Series no 183) Foreign Policy Association. 345 E. 46th St. New York 10017. Je. '67.

Rostow, W. W. The stages of economic growth: a non-Communist manifesto. Cambridge University Press. '60.

*Schneider, R. M. Latin American panorama. (Headline Series no 178) Foreign Policy Association. 345 E. 46th St. New York 10017. Ag. '66.

Shonfield, Andrew. The attack on world poverty. Random House. '60.

Sigmund, P. E. ed. The ideologies of the developing nations. Praeger. '67.

Staley, Eugene. The future of the underdeveloped countries; political implications of economic development. Harper. '61.

Szulc, Tad. The winds of revolution: Latin America today—and tomorrow. Praeger. '65.

*Thant. The United Nations development decade at mid-point. United Nations. '65.

United Nations. The problems and policies of economic development: an appraisal of recent experience. World economic survey: 1967—part one. United Nations. '68.

United Nations. The United Nations and social development. United Nations. '66.

United Nations. Conference on Trade and Development, Geneva, 1964. Trade expansion and economic co-operation among developing countries; report of the Committee of Experts [José Garrido Torres, chairman]. United Nations. '66.

*United Nations. Economic and Social Council. Problems of plan implementation: development planning and economic integration in Africa. United Nations. '68.

United States. Congress. House of Representatives. Committee on Foreign Affairs. Subcommittee on Foreign Economic Policy. The involvement of U.S. private enterprise in developing countries. Supt. of Docs. Washington, D.C. 20402. '68.

Ward, Barbara. The lopsided world. Norton. '68.
Waterston, Albert. Development planning: lessons of experience. Johns Hopkins Press. '65.
Weiner, Myron, ed. Modernization: the dynamics of growth. Basic Books. '66.
Wilcox, W. A. India and Pakistan. (Headline Series no 185) Foreign Policy Association. 345 E. 46th St. New York 10017. O. '67.
Wolf, Charles. Foreign aid: theory and practice in southern Asia. Princeton University Press. '60.

## PERIODICALS

Africa Report. 13:7-15. Mr. '68. Tunisia modernizes. C. F. Gallagher.
African Affairs. 65:1-14. Ja. '66. Development and trade in Africa. R. K. A. Gardiner.
America. 113:496-8. O. 30, '65. New era in world development. C. H. Malik.
America. 117:538. N. 11, '67. Challenge to the opulent nations; summary of address. G. Díaz Ordaz.
America. 118:562-81. Ap. 27, '68. Latin America in revolution; symposium.
    *Discussion.* 119:86-7. Ag. 17, '68.
America. 118:768. Je. 15, '68. Lopsided world; widening gap between the rich and poor nations.
Annals of the American Academy of Political and Social Science. 360:63-7. Jl. '65. Disparities in progress among nations. T. C. Mann.
Bulletin of the Atomic Scientists. 17:43-7. F. '61. Needs of new states: science, men and money. W. A. Lewis.
Bulletin of the Atomic Scientists. 24:16-22. Ja. '68. World free of want? excerpts from address. Gerard Piel.
Business Week. p 56-7. D. 26, '64. Can a poor nation grow on an empty stomach?
Business Week. p 113. Ap. 17, '65. Hopes for harnessing the Mekong.
Business Week. p 109. D. 9, '67. Offering trade to the poor; system of tariff preferences to developing countries.
Business Week. p 88-9+. Mr. 16, '68. Can the poor lands bridge the gap?
Catholic World. 25:276-81. Ag. '67. Brazil's miserable northeast. H. W. Flannery.
Christian Century. 81:43-6. Ja. 8, '64. Population explosion demands worldwide action. J. A. O'Brien.
Christian Century. 83:745-8. Je. 8, '66. Trade and the war on world poverty. R. M. Fagley.

Christian Century. 84:1458-62. N. 15, '67. Prospects for population control. J. M. Stycos.

Christian Century. 85:71-4. Ja. 17, '68. Impasse in Latin America. A. H. Whiteford.

Christian Science Monitor. p 9. My. 27, '67. Latin American population spiral. J. N. Goodsell.

Christian Science Monitor. p 9. O. 27, '67. African student faces two worlds. Leonard Kibara.

Christian Science Monitor. p 8. D. 4, '67. 14 nations establish West African "EEC." R. W. Howe.

Commentary. 38:61-4. N. '64. Population myths. D. H. Wrong.

Commentary. 46:52-9. Jl. '68. Politics of development. J. P. Nettl and K. Von Vorys.

Commonweal. 85:226-8. N. 25, '66. Israel's aid to Africa. Gabriel Gersh.

Commonweal. 88:176-80. Ap. 26, '68. Incestuous dialogue; Christians and Marxists talk while the third world burns. Benjamin Page.

Current. 92:9-16. F. '68. Evolving Latin America.

Current. 95:52-5. My. '68. Changing world agriculture; excerpts from address, March 8, 1968. W. S. Gaud.

Current. 96:35-9. Je. '68. Controlling world population. P. R. Ehrlich.

Current. 96:48-52. Je. '68. Building new nations, compensation for the brain drain? W. C. Thiesenhusen.

Current History. 42:96-105+. F. '62. Development of Andean America. E. S. Urbanski.

Current History. 43:29-34+. Jl. '62. African problems of trade and aid. Arnold Rivkin.

Current History. 49:257-99+. N. '65. United States aid in Asia; symposium.

Current History. 50:22-6+. Ja. '66. Honduras: problems and prospects. W. S. Stokes.

Current History. 51:65-107+. Ag. '66. U.S. aid in a world setting; symposium.

Current History. 53:270-4+. N. '67. Progress in Venezuela. P. B. Taylor.

Daedalus. p 925-37. Summer '68. Underdevelopment, obstacles to the perception of change and leadership. A. O. Hirschmann.

Department of State Bulletin. 45:121-5. Jl. 17, '61. Problem of international economic imbalance; statement, June 19, 1961. G. W. Ball.

Department of State Bulletin. 45:233-8. Ag. 7, '61. Guerrilla warfare in the underdeveloped areas; address, June 28, 1961. W. W. Rostow.

Department of State Bulletin. 45:451-5. S. 11, '61. Importance of foreign aid in today's world; statement, August 21, 1961. Dean Rusk.

Department of State Bulletin. 49:712-21. N. 4, '63. Problems of economic development; statement, October 3, 1963. J. B. Bingham.

Department of State Bulletin. 49:806-10. N. 25, '63. Our obligation to the family of man; address, November 8, 1963. J. F. Kennedy.

Department of State Bulletin. 50:251-60. F. 17, '64. Challenge of democracy in developing nations; address, January 26, 1964. W. W. Rostow.

Department of State Bulletin. 51:664-9. N. 9, '64. Some lessons of economic development since the war; address, October 7, 1964. W. W. Rostow.

Department of State Bulletin. 52:104-7. Ja. 25, '65. Agricultural development in Africa; address, January 7, 1965. G. M. Williams.

Department of State Bulletin. 53:173-7. Jl. 26, '65. Challenge of the developing countries; address, May 23, 1965. D. E. Bell.

Department of State Bulletin. 53:709-16. N. 1, '65. Progress and problems in the Far East; address, October 5, 1965. W. P. Bundy.

Department of State Bulletin. 55:956-65. D. 26, '66. Impact of technology on world trade and economic development; addresses, November 16,1966. J. T. Connor; H. H. Humphrey.

Department of State Bulletin. 56:430-6. Mr. 13, '67. Improving export earnings of developing countries; statement, January 18, 1967. W. M. Blumenthal.

Department of State Bulletin. 57:534-40. O. 23, '67. Economic integration of Latin America; address, September 29, 1967. A. M. Solomon.

Department of State Bulletin. 58:238-42. F. 19, '68. Facts and ideas on industrialization; address December 1, 1967. W. M. Kotschnig.

Department of State Bulletin. 58:322-9. Mr. 4, '68. To build the peace: the foreign aid program for fiscal 1969; message, February 8, 1968. L. B. Johnson.

Department of State Bulletin. 58:359-68. Mr. 11, '68. From aid to cooperation: development strategy for the next decade; statement, February 5, 1968. E. V. Rostow.

Department of State Bulletin. 58:369-72. Mr. 18, '68. War on hunger; address at second international conference on the war on hunger, February 20, 1968. H. H. Humphrey.

Department of State Bulletin. 58:563-6. Ap. 29, '68. Political development and institution-building under the Alliance for Progress; address, April 8, 1968. C. T. Oliver.

Department of State Bulletin. 58:584-7. My. 6, '68. Integration and trade in the Alliance for Progress; address, April 9, 1968. C. T. Oliver.

Department of State Bulletin. 59:16-24. Jl. 1, '68. East Asia on the move; address, February 7, 1968. W. P. Bundy.

*Finance and Development (International Monetary Fund and World Bank). 5:2-9. S. '68. The ex-desert of Northwest Mexico. D. C. Fulton.

*Finance and Development (International Monetary Fund and World Bank). 5:13-17. S. '68. The world-wide opportunity for private capital. Abderrahman Tazi.

Foreign Affairs. 40:419-30. Ap. '62. Free Africa and the Common Market. Barbara Ward.

Foreign Affairs. 41:372-83. Ja. '63. Trade and the less developed areas. W. F. Butler.

Foreign Affairs. 41:536-49. Ap. '63. Latin America's troubled cities. C. M. Haar.

Foreign Affairs. 41:708-20. Jl. '63. Economic development through private enterprise. E. G. Collado.

Foreign Affairs. 42:242-54. Ja. '64. Aid, trade and economic development: the changing political context. Janez Stanovnik.

Foreign Affairs. 43:87-98. O. '64. Soviet policy in the developing countries. P. E. Mosely.

Foreign Affairs. 44:173-97. Ja. '66. Revolution in Latin America. G. C. Lodge.

Foreign Affairs. 44:206-15. Ja. '66. Development decade in the balance. G. D. Woods.

Foreign Affairs. 44:403-16. Ap. '66. What private enterprise means to Latin America. David Rockefeller.

Foreign Affairs. 44:601-61. Jl. '66. Aspects of development; symposium.

Foreign Affairs. 45:520-40. Ap. '67. New perspectives on trade and development. Isaiah Frank.

Foreign Affairs. 45:715-25. Jl. '67. U.S. assistance to less developed countries, 1956-65. K. M. Kauffman and Helen Stalson.

Foreign Affairs. 46:126-36. O. '67. Malnutrition and national development. A. D. Berg.

*Foreign Affairs. 46:167-80. O. '67. The population crisis: reasons for hope. F. W. Notestein.

*Foreign Affairs. 46:688-98. Jl. '68. The agricultural revolution in Asia. L. R. Brown.

Foreign Affairs. 46:758-69. Jl. '68. Two revolutions. D. C. Smith, Jr.

*Foreign Affairs. 47:138-50. O. '68. How India is tackling her population problem. S. Chandrasekhar.

Fortune. 72:164-9+. N. '65. South America's shattered showcase. Philip Siekman.

Fortune. 77:132-5+. My. '68. Dynamite in rising expectations. Max Ways.

Fortune. 77:104-13+. Je. 1, '68. Indonesia's potholed road back. Robert Lubar.

*Harper's Magazine. 237:64-75. S. '68. Making a rational foreign policy now. R. L. Heilbroner.

Harper's Magazine. 237:67+. D. '68. A warning to the rich white world. P. F. Drucker.

International Conciliation. 568:4-80. My. '68. UNCTAD: North-South encounter. Branislav Gosovic.

International Labor Review. 97:517-24. Je. '68. World employment program. D. A. Morse.

International Organization. 22:1-475. Winter '68. The global partnership: international agencies and international development; ed. by R. N. Gardner and M. F. Millikan.

Monthly Labor Review. 88:145-7. F. '65. Exporting U.S. standards to underdeveloped countries. J. C. Shearer.

Nation. 200:377-8; 380-97. Ap. 12, '65. Billion-dollar mystery; with editorial comment. F. J. Cook.

Nation. 200:414-17. Ap. 19, '65. Backward nations: aid and resources. W. C. Paddock and Paul Paddock.

Nation. 203:280-3. S. 26, '66. Latin America: economic integration for progress. F. G. Gil.

Nation. 205:549-50. N. 27, '67. Of, by and for the rich.

Nation. 205:594-6. D. 4, '67. Ignoring the storm warnings; causes of counterrevolution. G. H. C. Bing.

Nation. 206:685, 696-700. My. 27, '68. Aid and squeeze in Asia; with editorial comment. F. L. Starner.

National Geographic Magazine. 131:1-47. Ja. '67. Problems of a two-part land. Bern Keating.

Nation's Business. 52:38-9+. S. '64. How world trade will change.

Natural History. 77:6-8+. My. '68. Coming famine. P. R. Ehrlich.

New Republic. 152:13-14. Ap. 24, '65. On the Mekong; Mr. Johnson's billion-dollar offer. J. F. Ridgeway.

New Statesman. 72:512-14. O. 7, '66. Summing-up the debate on world hunger. Mervyn Jones.

New York Times. p 1+. Mr. 11, '68. Myrdal finds the outlook for South Asia is gloomy. Peter Kihss.

New York Times. p 1+. Ap. 16, '68. Hemisphere fails to meet year-old goal for growth. P. L. Montgomery.

New York Times. p 1. Ag. 7, '68. World Bank's aid to be increased to offset U.S. cut. E. L. Dale, Jr.

New York Times. p 1+. S. 8, '68. Many in India call for self-reliance as aid substitute. Joseph Lelyveld.

New York Times. p 73. S. 26, '68. Food hopes gain for poor nations. E. L. Dale, Jr.

New York Times. p 1+. O. 1, '68. McNamara, at World Bank, decries population boom. E. L. Dale, Jr.

*New York Times. p 58. O. 1, '68. Text of address by World Bank's new president. R. S. McNamara.

New York Times. p 1+. D. 26, '68. New investments in aid are sought; businessmen suggest U.S. agency to promote more private capital abroad. Felix Belair, Jr.

New York Times Magazine. p 22+. Ap. 16, '61. $2,700 a year or $70 a year. B. K. Nehru.

New York Times Magazine. p 10+. D. 17, '61. Selling a revolution to Latin America. Tad Szulc.

New York Times Magazine. p 15+. Ag. 25, '63. Another view of the Latin-American problem. J. P. Davies, Jr.

New York Times Magazine. p 35+. S. 29, '63. Handicap for new nations: climate. G. H. T. Kimble.

New York Times Magazine. p 9+. Jl. 12, '64. Foreign aid has succeeded. Barbara Ward.

New York Times Magazine. p 28-9+. Ja. 14, '68. It's God's will; why interfere? Joseph Lelyveld.

*New York Times Magazine. p 58-60+. O. 13, '68. Can India survive Calcutta? Joseph Lelyveld.

*Newsweek. 70:38-40. O. 30, '67. "Scandal of the century": rich and poor. Arnaud de Borchgrave.

Newsweek. 70:53. D. 11, '67. Seeds of hope; formation of the East African economic community.

OECD Observer (Organization for European Economic Co-operation and Development). p 14-20. S. '66. The financial terms of foreign aid: discipline or danger? R. E. Benedick.

Reader's Digest. 82:129-34. Mr. '63. Indonesia: time bomb in the South Pacific. W. J. Lederer and Eugene Burdick.

Reader's Digest. 88:139-44. F. '66. Formosa: Asia's heartening success story. Keyes Beech and C. W. Hall.

Reader's Digest. 89:203-4+. S. '66. Foreign aid that works. James Daniel.

Reader's Digest. 93:161-4+. S. '68. For the world's forgotten: a long-proven, down-to-earth program. C. W. Hall.

Reporter. 35:31-4. D. 1, '66. Bolivia: revolution in mid-passage. Gladys Delmas.

Reporter. 36:24. My. 18, '67. First steps toward an Asian Common market. Denis Warner.

Reporter. 37:35-6. D. 14, '67. India's haphazard birth-control program. G. W. S. Trow.

Round Table. 58:143-50. Ap. '68. Foreign aid in decline. J. C. Culver.

Saturday Evening Post. 236:34-6. N. 30, '63. Why can't we save Latin America? Richard Armstrong.

Saturday Review. 44:79-82. O. 14, '61. Need to give wisely. H. J. Morgenthau.

Saturday Review. 46:29-30. Ag. 17, '63. Education's role in the developing nations. P. H. Coombs.

Saturday Review. 48:10+. Ag. 14, '65. Behind the scenes in Vietnam; Asian development bank. Henry Brandon.

Saturday Review. 48:124-5. S. 18, '65. Press in developing countries. R. F. Rankin.

Saturday Review. 49:24. Jl. 30, '66. UNESCO and literacy: progress report. R. L. Tobin.

Saturday Review. 49:22-5. S. 17, '66. Rich and the poor: 1966. P. G. Hoffman.

Saturday Review. 50:24-6. Mr. 11, '67. The brain drain: how poor nations give to the rich. W. F. Mondale.

Saturday Review. 50:49-50. Ag. 19, '67. Global revolution. P. H. Coombs.

Science. 157:651-7. Ag. 11, '67. Health, population and economic development. C. E. Taylor and M. F. Hall.
  Reply. Science. 159:150. Ja. 12, '68. R. W. Tichauer.

Science. 158:730-9. N. 10, '67. Population policy: will current programs succeed? Kingsley Davis.

Science. 159:611-12+. F. 9, '68. Population control; U.S. aid program leaps forward. L. J. Carter.

Senior Scholastic. 89:15-17. O. 21, '66. Economic growth: key to the good life for all.

Senior Scholastic. 92:17. F. 29, '68. Economics & Asia.

Senior Scholastic. 92:17-18. F. 29, '68. Economics & Africa.

Senior Scholastic. 92:18. F. 29, '68. Economics & Latin America.

Sociology and Social Research. 52:193-202. Ja. '68. Concept of community in developing nations. A. K. Basu.

Time. 84:80+. Ag. 28, '64. Hard struggle; United Nations report on non-Communist Asia.

Time. 90:50+. O. 20, '67. Eye or the finger? conference on world crisis in education.

Time. 91:67-8. My. 31, '68. Perils & promise of peace.

Time. 92:68. Jl. 19, '68. Self-help with outside help; Asian development bank.

U.S. News & World Report. 51:62-4. Ag. 14, '61. Putting Latin America on the road to prosperity; interview. Raúl Prebisch.

U.S. News & World Report. 54:72-9. F. 11, '63. True story of black Africa and its future; interview. G. H. T. Kimble.

U.S. News & World Report. 54:77-9. My. 6, '63. Seven myths about Latin America. D. B. Richardson.

U.S. News & World Report. 55:60-4. S. 16, '63. Too many people in the world?

U.S. News & World Report. 60:70-2. Je. 6, '66. Indonesia: hope, where once there was none. R. P. Martin.

U.S. News & World Report. 61:98-101. O. 24, '66. Black Africa: free, but deep in trouble.

U.S. News & World Report. 61:68-71. N. 28, '66. India: a huge country on the verge of collapse. S. W. Sanders.

U.S. News & World Report. 63:74-6. S. 4, '67. New hope for India, but: still a nation on the brink.

U.S. News & World Report. 63:80-1. S. 4, '67. Problems of independence: a look at the third world; interview. B. Ben Yahmed.

U.S. News & World Report. 63:70-2+. S. 18, '67. Problems and progress in Latin America: a look ahead; interview. J. N. Wallace.

*U.S. News & World Report. 63:50-4. D. 25, '67. Indonesia: poor people in a rich land; first-hand report. J. N. Wallace.

U.S. News & World Report. 64:48-52. Mr. 11, '68. Amazing success story in Asia. Howard Handleman.

U.S. News & World Report. 65:76-8. Ag. 12, '68. Developing an Asian nation: test case in Indonesia. J. N. Wallace.

UNESCO Courier. 15:55-6. Jl; 17-22. S. '62. Anatomy of underdevelopment.

UNESCO Courier. 18:4-34. O. '65. Turning point; symposium.

UNESCO Courier. 19:23-4. Ap. '66. Education for a new agricultural revolution; UNESCO program.

UNESCO Courier. 20:28-36. Ag. '67. Development, new name for peace; excerpt from encyclical On the development of peoples. Paul VI, Pope.
    Reply, with title: To build a new order in the world. René Maheu. UNESCO Courier. 20:36-9. Ag. '67.

UNESCO Courier. 21:8+. Mr. '68. Bigger populations, less food. J. M. Van Gindertael.

UNESCO Courier. 21:13-16. Ap. '68. Literacy: the ABC of development.

United Nations Monthly Chronicle. 3:44-52. F. '66. Some fundamental problems of world trade. Raúl Prebisch.

United Nations Monthly Chronicle. 5:39-40. F. '68. Advisory mission on family planning to Pakistan; joint UN-WHO mission.

United Nations Review. 10:12-14. Ap. '63. International aspects of development; address, April 5, 1963. Thant.
United Nations Review. 10:13-21. My. '63. Toward a dynamic development policy for Latin America. Raúl Prebisch.
United Nations Review. 11:31-4+. Mr. '64. Housing needs in the Development Decade.
Vital Speeches of the Day. 27:315-18. Mr. 1, '61. Under-developed world today; address, January 13,1961. B. K. Nehru.
Vital Speeches of the Day. 28:395-7. Ap. 15, '62. Development policies; address, March 2, 1962. J. A. Mayobre.
Vital Speeches of the Day. 34:536-8. Je. 15, '68. Economic development, key to the world's future; address, May 9, 1968. R. M. Allan, Jr.
Washington Post. p B3. Mr. 10, '68. The fight against hunger is already lost. Paul Ehrlich.
Western Political Quarterly. 19:719-32. D. '66. Effects of corruption in a developing nation. D. H. Bayley.
World Health. p 3-5. Jl. '68. Africa at the crossroads. Alfred Quenum.
World Health. p 6-10. Jl. '68. The crucial problem.
World Justice. 7:308-35. Mr. '66. The United Nations and the decade of development. Barbara Ward.
World Today. 22:142-51. Ap. '66. In defense of development. I. S. Friedman.